The Salvation
of the LORD

The Salvation
of the LORD

Michael L. White

Parson Place Press
Mobile, Alabama

The Salvation of the LORD, 2nd Edition, Revised and Expanded by Michael L. White

Cover image, design and production courtesy of Canva.com.

ISBN: 978-0-9888528-8-4
Library of Congress Control Number: 2022913466

Dedication

To my Beloved Lord Jesus, who saved me by His precious, atoning blood and His wonderful, matchless grace!

Other Titles by This Author

Digital Evangelism: You Can Do It, Too!

A Time for Everything:
The Kevin Zimmerman Story

Seven Keys to Effective Prayer

Lifelines

A Publishing Panacea:
How to Be Your Own Publisher in the Digital Age

Contents

ACKNOWLEDGMENTS

Naturally, I acknowledge that, without God, I could not possibly accomplish such a monumental task as explaining God's Plan of Salvation for humankind in such a limited volume as this. While I believe He provided a significant degree of inspiration to me during the composition of this book, I am certainly not claiming that what I've written here in any way approaches the level of Scripture. However, I am convinced that God gave me both the idea for writing this book and all the spiritual insight required to "rightly divid[e] the word of truth" (2 Timothy 2:15) during the writing and editing process for both the first and second editions. Thanks be to God for His indescribable grace!

I also want to thank those who have so graciously agreed to read and endorse this second edition. I know what busy lives you lead and how challenging it is to set aside time for such a project as this. Your personal favor is such a blessing to me! I pray that I will have the opportunity to bless you in a similar way before we leave this earth.

Finally, although it has taken much longer than I expected or intended to finally sit down and compose this second edition, I am relieved that I have finally finished it. Furthermore, I pray this book will have a tremendously positive impact on the spiritual life of everyone who reads it. If it succeeds in redirecting even one errant soul, it will have accomplished my goal and fulfilled my joy! As the Apostle James wrote, "Brethren, if anyone among you wanders from the truth, and someone turns him back, let him know that he who turns a sinner from the error of his way will save a soul from death and cover a multitude of sins" (James 5:19-20). Amen and amen!

FOREWORD

The topic of salvation is paramount not only for the global Christian church but for the entire human race. The reality of humanity's need for salvation is why I originally involved myself with ministry efforts as a young man and is the chief motivation for my ministry now as a lead pastor. Growing up in church, I was well-acquainted with certain aspects of the faith and would have even considered myself well-versed on the subject of salvation. However, it was in my early twenties that I was truly confronted with the awe-inspiring revelation that God not only has a will and a plan to save me from the destruction that I very much deserve, but He also wishes me to be an instrument of His salvation for the lost world around me. This epiphany occurred because of me being challenged in my faith to read through the entire Bible from cover to cover. It was through reading of the fullness of God's plan for myself, the majestic foreshadowing of His redemption in the Old Testament and the epic revealing of the Christ as His mechanism of both justice and mercy, that I truly became compelled to action and embarked upon the mission of reaching the lost. The centerpiece of the Gospel, or "good news," is salvation—that a gracious God gave us His Son as the sacrifice for our sins, and through repentance and faith, we can enter eternal life. There is no truth more delightful, no message more compelling, and no single thing more important than seeing and understanding God's beautiful plan of salvation.

In the years that I have known Pastor Michael L. White, I have been blessed to encounter his discerning spiritual acumen, as well as learn from his vast knowledge of the Bible. Our conversations are always enlightening as they are usually composed mostly of discussion surrounding God's Word and the Christian life. This book offers an in-depth explanation of perhaps the most important doctrine of the Christian faith. Observe how Pastor White systematically breaks down salvation and takes you on a journey of discovering the wonderful doctrine of Soteriology. Carefully thought-out, this book takes an extensive look at all things related to being saved. Pastor Mike tastefully and tactfully handles even the most controversial of subjects, such as apostasy, predestination, and evolution, while maintaining a faithfulness to the inspired Word of God. Be sure to take extra time, if possible, to study the many biblical cross-references dispersed all throughout the book for your own personal enrichment.

You are now beginning a voyage through one of life's most important topics. May God bless you in this endeavor as you discover the beauty that is salvation!

Reverend Jacob Maloney
Lead Pastor of The Cross Church of Mobile, Alabama

INTRODUCTION

Not long after I had published the first edition of this book, I realized I had made a major error in forgetting to include a discussion about the doctrine of apostasy. However, both personal and professional pursuits delayed me from completing this second edition until now. Therefore, I am presenting this second edition as both a revised and expanded version, since, in addition to including a chapter on the doctrine of apostasy, I also made other editorial changes to clarify my previous commentary and correct a couple of mistakes I made.

Having now explained my purpose for composing this second edition, let me further state that it has been my goal in *both* editions to illuminate for the reader the essentiality of spiritual salvation and the necessity of understanding it God's way. In other words, not only must we perceive and accept that spiritual salvation is a requirement for spending eternity with the One True God, but we must comprehend and accept this salvation according to God's divine plan as laid out in the Judeo-Christian Scriptures of *The Holy Bible*. In fact, the very first obstacle we must overcome in this quest is whether to accept and believe in the Bible as God's divinely inspired

Word. If we reject its divine inspiration, which the Bible clearly claims for itself (see 2 Timothy 3:16 and 1 Peter 1:21), then we have ended our journey after taking only one step.

In the ensuing pages of this book, I hope to convince the reader that, since *The Holy Bible* is indeed inspired by God's Holy Spirit, not only *can* we trust its every word, but we *must* trust its every word if we are to be saved according to God's plan. Therefore, if we attempt to pick-and-choose what we wish to believe from the Bible, we tragically cut ourselves off from God's plan and doom our souls to Hell. For instance, trying to claim that Jesus can save us when we reject any aspect of His existence, character or atoning work as defined in the Bible, such as His divine Sonship, dual divine-human constitution, virgin birth, physical death on a Roman cross, and/or His physical resurrection from the dead, then our faith is futile, and we are still in our sins, as the Apostle Paul warns us in 1 Corinthians 15:17. Furthermore, I personally believe the same is true if we reject other portions of Scripture and try to revise them into secularly acceptable versions, such as amending the creation story by trying to syncretize the impossible-to-prove evolutionary theory with the biblical account of creation. By revising or amending *anything* as it is described for us in the Bible, including explaining away the historical events of the Global Flood and the Red Sea crossing as happening any other way than detailed for us in the Bible, we not only err, but we call God a liar to His face. As the Apostle Paul also wrote, "Indeed, let God be true but every man a liar" (Romans

3:4). So, as we begin our expedition and seek the salvation of the LORD that we all so desperately need, let us start by asking some fundamental questions.

Are you saved? In other words, have you received the salvation of the LORD? Whether you answer yes or no, do you understand what it truly means to "be saved"? You may be asking about now, "Saved from *what*–and *for* what?" This may very well be the best question of all to answer. Indeed, that is precisely the question at the center of why I have authored this book. These are all thought-provoking questions, but we can accurately answer them only after understanding the concept of spiritual salvation–that is, what it is and why it is necessary. In fact, until you understand what spiritual salvation is and why you personally need it, you will never desire it or even be able to receive it.

So, what *is* the salvation of the LORD, anyway, and why write an entire book on the subject? Well, in the simplest terms, the salvation of the LORD is a rescue from the punishment of Hell, which every human being is subject to because of sin. Of course, that begs a whole series of other questions, such as "What is sin?", "What is Hell?", "Why does Hell exist?", and, perhaps most importantly, "How can a God described as Love even create such a place as Hell, let alone send anyone there?" Thus, when I considered authoring a book on this subject, I wanted to try to cover everything that I thought pertinent to the discussion, beginning with the character of God. After all, I believe an accurate understanding of God's character is essential to understanding why such a thing as spiritual salvation is necessary and why it must be accepted just as it is.

Whether you're simply a curious onlooker wondering if there really could be anything to this notion of only One True God and eternal life after death, or whether you're a member of another (non-Christian) religion who wants to compare beliefs, or whether you're a Christian believer who is looking for some reinforcement to your own thinking about the salvation of the LORD, this book is especially for you. It is intended for *anyone* who is even a little bit interested in what the salvation of the LORD is, how you can obtain it, and how you can be *sure* you have obtained it.

While covering this very important topic, I have used *The Holy Bible* as the primary source for everything I've written about God, Jesus, salvation, eternal life, Heaven and Hell, and everything related to them, so you won't find many extra-biblical references herein, except for those dictionaries and other related scholarly sources which help to clarify the actual meaning of words in the original Bible languages of Hebrew and Greek, as well as in today's English. I prefer to let the Bible speak for itself and even interpret itself where an actual interpretation is available, but where a direct interpretation is not available, these other sources serve as a scholarly foundation, or even an outside reinforcement, to my own interpretations.

Naturally, since I am a fallible human being (like you) you can easily dismiss my interpretations, but if you dismiss the clearly divine assertions as plainly revealed, self-interpreted, and written in the Bible, you should beware of the eternal consequences of doing so. Before you dismiss *anything* contained in the Bible, you should first ask yourself this important question: "What might be the consequences of rejecting this idea, either in the here and now or in the afterlife?" I urge you to consider just these two alternatives before making up your mind to reject anything in the Bible: if the Bible is wrong in its assertions about God, the universe, and the afterlife, then you risk nothing at all by rejecting its commands, but if the Bible is *right* in its presentation, then by rejecting these truths, you have forfeited your eternal soul and the hope of everlasting life with the one and only True God, the most benevolent Being ever to exist.

You see, this is no light decision. Your eternal soul literally hangs in the balance. It is a little like making a life-or-death decision for your physical wellbeing, such as attempting to disarm the complex electrical wiring to a cleverly devised time bomb. Which wire must you snip to disconnect the bomb from its timing detonator? The time is quickly ticking down while you try to decide. You are down to a choice between the red wire and the green wire. If you snip the wrong wire, the bomb will detonate. Which one is the right one? Which one will *you* choose?

This sort of analogy may also help with choosing which truth to trust in. The fact is that there really is only one truth, but there is another source claiming to be the truth as well. Like the proverbial evil twin trying to deceive us, how can we discern which one is the *true* truth? It is a fact, however, that even identical twins are not absolutely identical, so it is just a matter of knowing the difference between the two and choosing the one with the characteristics that match the correct one.

How can we know for sure that the Bible is the truth? For me, it is a matter of comparing the Bible's truth with what I see in the world around me. If it lines up with verifiable reality, then I know it is the truth. Just like detecting that one physical or mental difference between the good and evil twins, this is that one difference between the truth and the pretend truth. Moreover, since I have personally experienced the evidential existence and presence of God via answered prayer, and since the Bible purports to be the absolute truth from God's own mouth with absolutely no error, then if something appears *not* to match up with reality, I re-examine it from as many other perspectives as I can to ascertain the truth. In those cases where I have yet been unable to explain a conflict between the Bible's assertion and my perception of reality, I have made it a matter of faith to believe the Bible. Because of God's integrity, I believe I can trust what He says in the Bible. Like the sometimes-comical query, "Have I ever lied to you?" when we are asked to trust another's word, God wants us to consider whether we can trust *His* Word. It is no laughing matter if God should ask this question, however, because not only has He never lied to us, but it is *impossible* for God to lie (see Hebrews 6:18 and Titus 1:2)!

Since I have personally observed God at work in my own life, as well as in the lives of others, I can truthfully answer, "No," to this question of whether God has ever lied to me. Therefore, I have complete confidence that if God tells me in the Bible that something is true, then I can take it at face value, even if I cannot fully understand or explain it. I believe that if God has proven Himself trustworthy in other points, I can certainly trust Him with the facts I cannot yet comprehend or explain.

Every human being must make up his or her own mind about what to believe–and, yes, that includes you. Hopefully, after reading this book you will be in a better position to make your decision. If the Bible is true and there *is* such a reality as only One True God who created all things and inspired the writing of the Bible, then the consequence of rejecting that reality is beyond description. As awful as eternal Hell is, its reality is far beyond full comprehension. As wonderful as eternal Heaven is, its reality, too, is far beyond full comprehension. If you want to avoid Hell's reality and enjoy Heaven's reality, keep reading this book to the very end before you make your decision. Now, let us commence the quest.

CHAPTER ONE: THE CHARACTER OF GOD

Before we delve into the rest of this book, we should make a careful and considerate study of the character of God. By no means will we be able to fully explain or understand the entire character of God in this review, but we can, at least, demonstrate some of the primary points to God's character which the Bible reveals for us to help us better understand who God is, how He behaves and relates to His creation, and what He expects and requires of us. Without a proper knowledge and understanding of God, the remainder of this book's content may make little sense.

Of course, all that we can know about God is what we find written about Him (and certainly revealed and inspired *by* Him) in the Scriptures (*The Holy Bible*). Our experiences with God must therefore be a confirmation of what we read in the Bible. We must never reverse this process and attempt to make the Bible confirm our subjective experiences with God, since we can be easily deceived by evil spirits masquerading as good spirits from God (see 2 Corinthians 11:12-15). Tragically, this is what happened to Shirley McClain and

Oprah Winfrey, who were reportedly raised in presumably Christian homes, but as adults they were lured away from the truth of God's Word by seducing spirits spouting lies about God, His Son Jesus, and His Word. This has come to be known as "New Age" teaching, and it is complete heresy as compared to the Bible.

No other source besides the Bible is trustworthy for basing the salvation of one's soul. Though another source may contain a measure of wise instruction drawn from the truth of God's word, no other source can rightly claim direct inspiration by the One True God of all creation. To adopt this position on the Bible as the divinely revealed and inspired Word of God may require a certain measure of faith initially, but once one digs into the Scriptures and begins to realize the incontrovertible facts and truths contained therein, it becomes a bedrock foundation for peace of mind and confident living.

While other sources may contain elements of divine inspiration (i.e., truths set forth by the One True God in the Bible), none have the same forceful mandate for obedience as *The Holy Bible*, because God did not dictate every single word contained in these other writings to the attuned scribe who wrote them, and that certainly includes the book you are now reading. Thus, every book we read must be measured against the standard of truth contained in *The Holy Bible* to discern whether we may believe its contents or not. Any writing, including this book you are now reading, which contradicts what the Bible has already said about any subject is to be eschewed as false. It is entirely possible, however, for a useful book to contain both truth and falsehood (and not always *deliberately* false), so it is therefore the reader's responsibility to sort out the truth by consulting the holy Scriptures, that is, by using the holy Scriptures as the *standard* for truth.

One would not disregard a large diamond lying in a puddle of sewage simply because it was surrounded by disgusting refuse, nor would one cast away a diamond after close examination revealed a tiny speck of dung stuck to one of its many facets. By the same token, one would not deny the obvious truth of God's Word found amid a heretical work or cast aside an otherwise truthful work simply because it contained an erroneous thought within it. Nevertheless, a written work that is more falsehood than truth must be set aside as unreliable and even dangerous to the soul, though it may contain some elements of truth.

I say all this to emphasize that there is only one book in all human history that may be solely relied upon for absolute truth, and that book is *The Holy Bible*. If you deny and disregard everything I've written in this book you're now reading, you may yet return to the Bible for the final word in whatever discussion and consideration you may have. There, and there alone, is the inerrant and infallible Word of God to be found and followed. If we can't believe that about the Bible, then we can't be certain about anything else regarding God or our required faith in Him.

If you reject the inerrancy of the Word of God as contained in the Bible, however, you are left with no dependable means of discerning and sorting out the truth for *anything*, since everyone's words become equal and acceptable in the court of public opinion. You are, in effect, set adrift in a sea of ignorance and agnosticism filled with countless contradictions. If you cannot presently accept the basic and simple truth about the divine inspiration of the Bible as *the* literal Word of God, I urge you to keep an open mind about this aspect until you have finished reading this book. If you are truly willing to consider all possibilities in your quest for the truth, then perhaps you will be willing to reconsider your opinion of the Bible and its claim of divine inspiration. If you are willing to open your mind just enough to consider the possibility that you could be mistaken in your current conclusion about God and His Word, I encourage you to continue reading for further insight. With that in mind, let us now proceed with getting to know and understand God's true character as revealed to and for us in *The Holy Bible*.

God Is Righteous

According to Webster's online dictionary, the word *righteous* means "acting in accord with divine or moral law : free from guilt or sin."[1] Of course, the "divine or moral law" was instituted by God Himself. Being "free from guilt or sin" means either one has not violated the divine or moral law which God has instituted or one has been absolved of guilt via some means of atonement. The main problem which the second part of this definition overlooks is that once one has violated God's moral law, he or she must atone for that and every subsequent violation before he or she can be truly "free from guilt or sin." Unfortunately, this leaves the violator in a rather hopeless situation, since one cannot atone for his or her own sin. Only another sinless (i.e., guiltless) human being can make a sinner righteous by substituting His own righteousness for the sinner's *unrighteousness*.

This leads us to the first characteristic of God that we will consider. God is righteous. *Righteous* is also synonymous with *just*, from which we get the word *justice*. In other words, before justice can be attained, what is wrong must be made right. *Just* is also the root for the word *justified*, which means *to make right or righteous*. Therefore, justice is served when what was done wrong (the violation of the law) is justified (made right through an act of atonement). While this process is accomplished in human courts by forcing the violator to pay for his or her own wrongdoing, either by a monetary fine, or with time served in jail, or both, sometimes one may be required to pay for taking another's life by forfeiting his or her own life. Atonement is not as simple in the divine court of Almighty God, however.

God is righteous, not because He is justified (made right), but because He has never violated His Word, which also doubles for His Law. Therefore, God is righteous because He is a Person of His Word. In other words, if God says He will do something, He does it not only because it is the right thing to do, but because He *said* He would do it, and He doesn't hold us to a different standard than He holds Himself. Furthermore, as He said through the writer of the book of Hebrews in the New Testament of the Bible (who I personally believe to be the Apostle Paul), ". . . it *is* impossible for God to lie . . ." (Hebrews 6:18). Thus, as that very passage in Hebrews 6:18 is stating, because it is impossible for God to lie, God's Word *cannot* be broken, so when God swears that He will do something, He is taking an already assured feat to the next level of assurance! It ought to be enough for any of us to believe that if God says it that settles it. However, when God wants to assure us even more, He swears by His own most holy name, since there is nothing greater than Himself. If it was impossible for God to lie about anything in the first place, having God not only say that He will do something but to *swear* that He will do it makes the impossible even *more* impossible! Did you get that?

A former parishioner of mine used to visit me in my church office regularly and sit for a while to discuss whatever was on his mind at the time. He would sometimes question and sometimes challenge statements I had made in my sermon the previous Sunday. After I had offered clarification of what I meant, he was usually satisfied. Along with these occasionally deep discussions of theology and quests for how to live out the Christian life daily, he oftentimes got into some other matters of thought which were just as worthy of consideration. On more than one occasion he would begin a sentence with, "To be honest, . . ." and then pause to say, "Doesn't that sound strange to start off that way? I mean, aren't we *always* supposed to be honest?" I would usually smile and nod approvingly, while waiting for him to proceed with his thought.

I can't recall if I ever commented to him about this insight, but I have thought about it somewhat since departing from my pastoral role there. It has occurred to me that Jesus often began His teaching with phrases like "Truly, Truly, . . ." or "I tell you the truth. . . ." Isn't that equivalent to our phrase, "To be honest, . . ." or "Honestly . . ."? I think it is. So, why does Jesus say that? Perhaps He says it for the same reason God swore by His own holy name in the Old Testament Scriptures: to reinforce an already undeniable truth and to confirm an already unbreakable promise.

Thus, the fact of being righteous and unable to lie or break His Word, God is therefore limited in how He can speak or act. In other words, He cannot say anything that contradicts something else He has spoken, nor can He *do* anything that contradicts or breaks anything else He has spoken. To do so would make Him into a liar. As the Apostle Paul wrote, ". . . let God be true but every man a liar" (Romans 3:4).

When I was a student in high school, a fellow student of mine once played a trick on me with a word game. Because I had a reputation throughout my school for being a committed Christian, and I was even elected for my junior and senior years as the student council chaplain, he asked me, "Can God do anything?" I took the bait and said unhesitatingly, "Yes!" His quick retort was then, "Can He make a rock so big He can't lift it?" As he broke into howls of laughter at my mental predicament for having no good answer, I was left to ponder the correct answer to his original question, "Can God do anything?" The right answer, of course, is "No. Since God cannot sin or otherwise contradict His own Word, God cannot do just *anything*." Therefore, when Jesus says, ". . . with God all things are possible," (Matthew 19:26; Mark 10:27; which is what I was basing my original response upon) we are to presume that He is speaking within the confines of God's righteous Word. All things are possible with God, and yet it is *impossible* for Him to lie (or to commit *any* sin, for that matter), so how can both these statements be absolutely true? Anything is possible with God within the truth of His Word, but once we step outside of His Word, we enter the realm of the truly impossible. When we step outside of God's truth and His Plan of Salvation for us, even God Almighty cannot help us without violating His own Word, and He will *never* do that.

The fact is that God has made a way of escape from the throes of sin upon our souls, but He leaves the choice up to us whether to take it. If we do not take God at His word and accept His offer of salvation, we are truly doomed forever, because **God's Plan of Salvation is Plan A, and there *is no* Plan B.**

God Is Omniscient

The word *omniscient* is another way of saying *all-knowing*. God is all-knowing. Where do we get that notion? Well, the Bible, of course! Three key passages which inform us of this aspect of God's character are found in Isaiah 46:9-10, Psalm 139:1-2, and Luke 12:6-7. First, God says through His prophet Isaiah (46:9-10),

> Remember the former things of old, For I *am* God, and *there is* no other; *I am* God, and *there is* none like Me, Declaring the end from the beginning, And from ancient times *things* that are not *yet* done, Saying, "My counsel shall stand, And I will do all My pleasure, . . ."

"Declaring the end from the beginning. . . ." *That's* omniscience. I liken this to a favorite movie you have watched repeatedly, so that you know the final line from the closing scene, even as the opening credits are showing on the screen. Nevertheless, even that is not technically telling the future, because you have no idea whether the power may go out while you're watching the movie or whether some mishap may interrupt the movie during viewing or any number of other interferences that simply can't be foreseen without the power of omniscience.

How can anyone know the future well enough to foretell precisely what will happen, and in the order it will happen, even a few seconds into the future, let alone many years in advance? Yet God tells the people of Israel (and us via the Scriptures) exactly what to expect many years, and in many cases *millennia*, into the future from their time. In fact, many of the events God foretold in the Scriptures more than 2,500 years ago are only just now coming to pass in our time. Other events happened within a few years of the time He foretold them to Israel to give them a proof that He knew what He was talking about. For instance, God foretold through His

prophet Daniel about the rise and fall of three more empires following Babylon. Daniel's precision was so accurate that for centuries some unbelieving scholars doubted the efficacy of his book.
They put forth the prospect that the book of Daniel was written *after* all those events happened, because it was simply too precisely
accurate to have been written beforehand! It was not until the infamous Dead Sea scrolls discovery that an *earlier* copy of the book
of Daniel was found in that collection, intact and practically indis-
tinct from the *later* source copy of Daniel that Bible scholars had
used for translation for centuries. Not only had God inspired His
Word, but He had preserved it as well. Imagine that!

The second verse of Scripture which informs us of God's omniscience is found in Psalm 139:1-2, where David says,

> O LORD, You have searched me and known *me*. You
> know my sitting down and my rising up; You under-
> stand my thought afar off.

In this passage, David is saying that God is intimately familiar
with his innermost thoughts! In fact, we might even interpret
the statement "You understand my thought afar off" as "You
know my thoughts even before I think them!" Now *that's* omniscience! Does that psalm refer only to God's knowledge of David,
or does it include us, too? It includes every human being that
has ever lived on this planet, and that means us as well!

Now, the third passage of Scripture which informs us of God's
omniscience is spoken by none other than Jesus, who (according to

John 1:1 & 14 & 1 Timothy 3:16) is God in human flesh. It is found in Luke 12:6-7:

> "Are not five sparrows sold for two copper coins? And not one of them is forgotten before God. But the very hairs of your head are all numbered. Do not fear therefore; you are of more value than many sparrows."

Knowing the number of hairs on any one person's head would be a phenomenal feat, but to know it for every human being who has ever lived is beyond human comprehension. How do we know that God knows this about *everyone*? We know it because Jesus was speaking to a crowd when He said it. Therefore, we can know that this assertion applies to *all* people. Now *that's* omniscience!

Knowing the end from the beginning, knowing our thoughts beforehand, and knowing exactly how many hairs are on our head at any given time, multiplied by billions of people who are living, or who have ever lived, ought to be proof enough of God's omniscience, even for the most dubious. The only ones who will continue to doubt in the face of such proof are those who flatly refuse to believe. It is for these that I believe the adage was coined: "There are none so blind as those who *will* not see."

God Is Omnipresent

The word omnipresent means "all-present" or "present everywhere at once." The Bible tells us God is omnipresent in Psalm

139:7-10, the same psalm where David proclaimed God's omnis-cience. In verses 7-10, David wrote:

> Where can I go from Your Spirit? Or where can I flee from Your presence? If I ascend into heaven, You *are* there; If I make my bed in hell, behold, You *are there*. *If* I take the wings of the morning, *And* dwell in the ut-termost parts of the sea, Even there Your hand shall lead me, And Your right hand shall hold me.

What David is saying, in effect, is there is no place to depart or hide from God's presence. This essentially means that God is everywhere we are. As Christians, this is especially notable when we consider that God sees and knows all about us, because He is always present with us. The Christian who yields to the tempta-tion to commit fornication should remind himself or herself that God is present with them, even in their throes of sinful passion. The Christian who chooses to lie on a regular basis has done so in the very presence of the living God who *always* knows the truth. The pastor (or any other church leader) and star choir so-loist who "fall in love" and sneak to the motel on the outskirts of town while their spouses are at work are committing adultery under the very watchful eye of the omnipresent God.

These are only a few examples, but I think you get the point. No one really stops to think about God's omnipresence and om-niscience when it comes to committing sin. They have deceived themselves into thinking that if they can hide their secret sins from everyone else, they can hide them from God. This could not be fur-ther from the truth.

Of course, we would all much rather contemplate God's omnipresence when considering how to escape from an especially trying circumstance. The lone hiker, for instance, who falls over a cliff into a tree-shrouded ravine far from civilization and any expectation of getting help can take comfort in the knowledge that God is not only present with him, but God is ready, able, and willing to help him get back to safety, if he will only trust Him. The same is true in the spiritual sense. When a believer wanders away from God's truth (His Word) and violates it, God, in His omnipresence and omniscience, calls him out and brings him back home, if he is willing. As King David said in Psalm 139:7-10, there really is no place we can go from the presence of God.

God Is Omnipotent

The word *omnipotent* means *all-powerful*. We often use another word for this, which also serves as a title for God. We use the title *God Almighty*. By using this title, we are saying that there is no one more powerful than God. This title, and the belief that goes with it, often brings up the complaint that either God doesn't truly care about people who experience calamities in their lives or else He isn't truly omnipotent after all. Such claims are rooted in ignorance of the true character of God. As I've already explained, God is restricted by His own Word so that He cannot act against it or break it in any way. I also cover some of these limitations as hindrances to our prayers in my book *Seven Keys to Effective Prayer*, which I also recommend to you.

God is indeed omnipotent, and He cares deeply for His people. He also cares for the unbelievers in this world, yet He cannot violate His Word to intervene for or spare those who refuse to abide by and in His Word. It really is just that simple. If you're looking for someone to blame for suffering in this world, don't blame God. Blame Satan, since he initiated this condition that we now know all too well as sin, which produces nothing but evil.

God Is Eternal

Eternity is one of the most difficult concepts for people to grasp, because it means having neither beginning nor end. The Scripture which explains this best about God is found in Psalm 90:2. This is the only psalm attributed to Moses, and it states:

> Before the mountains were brought forth, Or ever You had formed the earth and the world, Even from everlasting to everlasting, You *are* God.

A few other passages which depict this eternal existence of God are found in 1 Chronicles 16:36 and in Psalms 41:13, 103:17, and 106:48. You may notice in these verses that in some cases the translators insert the word *be* after the word *blessed*, while in other cases they insert the word *is*. Although they've done this to correct sentence structure in English, since the original Hebrew did not contain a word to translate in these cases, they've actually sacrificed clarity of meaning when they used the phrase "blessed *be* the LORD. . . ." I think the word *is* makes more sense in the context of these verses, however, because they're speaking of a God who *is* "from everlasting to everlasting" not One who *could be* "from everlasting to everlasting."

Since God is "from everlasting to everlasting," His attributes are likewise everlasting. A couple of these attributes I'd like to note here are His wisdom and His Word. Throughout Proverbs 8, wisdom is personified in the feminine and describes herself as having "been established from everlasting, From the beginning" (v. 23). That means the wisdom of God has always existed with Him. I strongly recommend you re-read that chapter, before you continue here.

Next, in John 1:1-3 and 14, we learn:

> In the beginning was the Word, and the Word was with God, and the Word was God. He was in the beginning with God. All things were made through Him, and without Him nothing was made that was made. . . . And the Word became flesh and dwelt among us, and we beheld His glory, the glory as of the only begotten of the Father, full of grace and truth.

Just like wisdom, God's Word has always existed with Him, but what makes this attribute even more powerful is the fact that God *incarnated* His Word (i.e., put it into flesh) in the Person of Jesus Christ. Therefore, Jesus is God in human flesh through the power and presence of His holy Word. Perhaps God conveyed His Word into the Virgin Mary's womb with the Hebrew equivalent of just one word: **CONCEIVE** (*harah*; pronounced hah-RAH Strong's H2029; הָרָה).[2]

"From everlasting to everlasting" means having neither beginning nor end. This means there has never been a time when God, with all His divine attributes, did not exist, nor will there ever be a time when God, with all His divine attributes, does *not* exist. Since everything we know, including ourselves, has both a beginning and an end (except God, of course), this is especially challenging for us to understand. The good news here is that, like so many other facts, we don't have to fully understand this truth to accept it.

God Is Slow to Anger

There are several passages of Scripture that tell us about God's slowness to become angry. Interestingly, those which contain the actual phrase "slow to anger" are found entirely in the Old Testament—that portion of Scripture everyone tends to associate with "a vengeful God"—rather than the gracious, merciful and forgiving God that He is and has always been (read Nehemiah 9:17; Psalm 103:8; Psalm 145:8; Joel 2:13; Jonah 4:2; and Nahum 1:3). God didn't suddenly develop grace, love, and mercy when Jesus came into the world, as so many misguided people seem to think. A careful reading of John 1:17 informs us that "the law was given through **Moses**, *but* grace and truth came through Jesus Christ [emphasis added]." If Jesus is God in human flesh, as John 1:1-3 & 14 and John 14:8-11 tell us, then God has *always* been the way Jesus portrays Him to be.

In times past, this aspect of God's character was arguably one of the most overlooked or ignored of all. Unfortunately, too many people, especially within the Church, have focused (in the past, at least) too much on God's righteous indignation and judgment and not enough on His grace and mercy. This description of God pushed many people *away* from God, rather than *toward* Him, tragically. Nowadays, however, it would seem the pendulum has swung the other way, and too many people, even within the Church, are focusing too much upon the grace and mercy of God to the exclusion of His righteous indignation and judgment so that we find churchgoers actively and openly engaging in sinful deeds while trusting in the grace and mercy of God to let them get by with it.

Both these extremes present an inaccurate picture of God's true character. We need to find the balance in our understanding of God that already exists in His divine character.

It is true that God is slow to anger and full of love, grace and mercy. This, of course, is God's preferred manner of relating to all in His creation, but the problem of sin (which we'll discuss in more detail in the next chapter) provokes God to anger, albeit slowly. The fact that God is *slow* to anger, however, does not mean that He doesn't *ever* get angry. What makes God angry? Impenitent sinners make God angry (i.e., those who persist unswervingly in their sins).

God always gives us ample opportunity to repent of our sins before He renders judgment and administers chastening. This is what is meant by the statement that God is slow to anger. God is much like a loving parent in this regard, and we are like the child going through the "terrible twos" defying and/or ignoring most of what God warns and says to us. While God will let us disobey Him for a season, giving us time and opportunities to repent of (or turn away from) our disobedience, He will eventually grow angry, not only over our act of disobedience, but because of our refusal to repent. In fact, I believe our refusal to repent makes God angrier than the sin we commit in the first place! The child who is swift to confess (admit) wrongdoing and repent (cease doing it) will receive far lesser chastisement from the parent (perhaps getting by with a firm warning not to repeat it) than the child who willfully continues in the wrongdoing and then tries to deny it when confronted in the act.

The fact that God is slow to anger is not something to be exploited, but it *is* something to be thankful for and appreciate. Remember that God is omniscient (that is, He knows *everything*, including the attitudes and intents of our hearts), so the one who willfully tries to exploit God's forbearance may raise God's ire all-the-sooner. Praise God for His love, grace, and mercy, but don't cheapen it by skirting in and out of God's favor through willful sin with the misunderstanding that God's slowness to anger will continue to let you by indefinitely. The day of chastening *will* come eventually–if we don't repent.

God Is Generous

While this characteristic of God does not need much definition, it certainly needs some clarification, even from people who are supposed to be children of God. Most people think they understand the meaning of the word *generous*, but they really understand only one aspect of generosity.

According to Merriam-Webster, the word *generous* means: "liberal in giving . . . marked by abundance or ample proportions."[3] This is the definition that most people might use, and while this is true in one aspect, there is another aspect in which one who is generous in giving is one who does not hesitate to give when presented with a request, regardless of the pool of resources at his or her disposal.

Notice I said *request* and not *need*. Many people fail to be generous because they want to justify their gift in accordance with a need, rather than a request. I have found that I have fallen into this snare more often than I care to admit. The fact is that a request includes both needs and unnecessary desires, but we tend to separate needs (such as things necessary to sustain life, health and safety) and requests (such as things that don't *necessarily* sustain life, health and safety). What holds most people back from giving then is basically only one of two things: greed or fear. Someone who is greedy will withhold giving simply because he or she doesn't want to share with anyone else, regardless of the circumstance or the pool of resources available to him or her. People who are fearful, however, are usually convinced they will be unable to replenish the resource pool from which they intend to give. If they fear depleting this pool beyond their ability to replenish it, they will withhold their giving, claiming quite sincerely that they can't spare anything for anyone else, lest they fail to have enough for themselves. The problem with this thinking is that *none* of us can maintain the resource pool from which we draw. So, we're relying upon the wrong source when we let this thinking dictate our level of generosity. Our resource pool is not our true source; our income from employment is not our true source; our income from investments is not our true source; but *God* is our *True Source.*

Perhaps you've heard the oft-repeated statement, "You can't out-give God," but do you know why that statement is true? First, are you sure it *is* true? Even if you aren't quite sure it is true, once I explain *why* it is true, perhaps you will be able to accept it as truth.

The reason we can't out-give God is because He gives first, and then He gives last. What does that mean? It means that everything we receive in our lives, including money, possessions, spouses, children, and much more, we receive first from the hand of God. The money we thought we earned from the job we "just happened" to find came from God, because God directed our steps to the point where we would be in the right place at the right time to get the tip from a friend or see the "Help Wanted" sign or meet the person doing the hiring so that we could get the job. He then gave us the health and the intellect to do the job day after day until payday. The possessions that we bought would not have been ours but for the money we earned from the job that we "just happened" to discover. The spouse that we married and the children that we produced together would not have entered our lives without the direction of God to bring us together and grant us fertility. Therefore, everything we have in life comes from God, because He gave first. This is true, of course, whether one is in covenant with God or not. However, there is a bonus for those who are in covenant with God. I'll explain more about that in a moment.

So, how does God give last? Well, that one is a little more complicated to explain, because it is based upon our response to God's initial gifts to us in the first place. Depending upon our level of generosity (i.e., our degree of imitating God in giving to others), God will multiply what we have so that He can give us even more. In fact, this principle of generosity is applicable whether one is in covenant with God or not. This explains why even unbelievers can amass great wealth, because they practice the principle of giving to others, whether unwittingly or not, and we must not forget that it is God who gives us the ability to gain wealth (Deuteronomy 8:18).

Once we become believers in covenant with God, however, matters become a bit more complicated. Whereas unbelievers can get away with not tithing to the ministry of God, so long as they are generous in giving to others (whether in need or simply to show favor), God will continue to bless and multiply their resources. On the other hand, as believers in covenant with God, our attitude toward the gifts that God gives us (i.e., whether we see them as gifts from God or something we earned or obtained on our own with no help from Him) has a direct impact on our level of personal resources.

Note that I am being careful to use the general term *resources* here, rather than money or finances alone. Our resources include much more than the amount of money we have in the bank. They also include our time, our possessions, our personal health, and anything else that God grants us in this world. Furthermore, the greater the amount we have of all these resources, the greater our level of personal prosperity. Now that word *prosperity* is another word which has been misunderstood and therefore misused and misapplied over the years. Mostly, we think only of finances when we think of prosperity, but according to the biblical understanding of the term (God's intended meaning, in other words), it means well-being in every aspect of our lives. In other words, we simply lack *nothing anywhere* in our lives. *That* is the bonus for believers in covenant with God which I mentioned a little earlier.

Now, what do I mean by "believers in covenant with God"? Isn't it enough simply to believe in God? Well, no, it isn't. Simply believing that God exists is only the beginning of what we are to believe. In fact, that is only the first step in coming to Him. As Hebrews 11:6 states:

> But without faith *it is* impossible to please *Him,* for he who comes to God must believe that He is [that He exists], and *that* He is a rewarder of those who diligently seek Him.

The Apostle James warns us with these words in his epistle:

> You believe that there is one God. You do well. Even the demons believe—and tremble! (James 2:19).

How many demons do you think God will allow to dwell with Him in His Eternal Kingdom? You see, demons don't have to be convinced that God is real to believe that He exists; they already *know* it! Neither are demons in covenant with God, which is the reason they won't be in His Eternal Kingdom.

So, what does it mean to be in covenant with God? Well, that's what this entire book is about. I'll explain more about that when we get to Chapter 11—So, How Can I *Know* I'm Saved?

God Is Merciful and Gracious

Of all the characteristics of God, these two may be the best known, even among those without a covenant with Him, and they are certainly the most abused by covenanters and non-covenanters alike. However, while most people think mercy and grace are synonymous, there is a fine distinction between them.

Although God's mercy is derived from His grace, it is not the same thing as His grace. Someone has defined mercy and grace this way: Mercy is *not getting* what we *do deserve* (punishment for our wrongdoing), while grace *is getting* what we *don't deserve* (forgiveness, salvation from Hell, and everlasting life in the Eternal Kingdom of Christ). I think that's a very apt and accurate definition.

If God was not filled with grace, however, He could and would have little or no mercy. His grace, of course, is based upon His great capacity for love. In fact, the Bible describes God *as* love (1 John 4:8 & 16). Therefore, when we read the description of the purest, highest kind of love in 1 Corinthians 13, we can understand why we simply can't measure up to it, because *God is love!*

It is precisely because of God's great love with which He has loved us (see Ephesians 2:4-9) that He is able to show us such great mercy and grace. Is this great love shown only to those who love and believe in Him? No, not according to what Jesus and the Apostle Paul have said.

> **For God so loved the world** that He gave His only be-gotten Son, that whoever believes in Him should not per-ish but have everlasting life (John 3:16; emphasis added).

> For scarcely for a righteous man will one die; yet per-haps for a good man someone would even dare to die. **But God demonstrates His own love toward us, in that while we were still sinners, Christ died for us** (Romans 5:7-8; emphasis added).

Furthermore, the Apostle Peter tells us:

> The Lord is not slack concerning *His* promise, as some count slackness, but is longsuffering toward us, not willing that any should perish but that all should come to repentance (2 Peter 3:9).

Therefore, God doesn't want to see any of us spend eternity in Hell, because of the great love He has for us. This has led the unrepentant and covenantal believers alike to display their igno-rance and ask, "So, why does God send *anyone* to Hell, if He doesn't really want *anyone* to go there?" The answer to this question is actually very simple. God doesn't *send* anyone to

Hell. People send themselves there *by choice* when they refuse to repent of their sins and accept the covenantal offer of salvation which God has made available through His Son Jesus Christ. You see, God has done everything for us except choose. He has left that one thing up to us. Several years ago, God gave me a rhyming couplet which I think explains this fact very well:

> God made the *provision*,
> But we must make the *decision*.

I'll say more about this in Chapter 11: So, How Can I *Know* I'm Saved?

God is Unchanging

Another hard-to-understand attribute of God's divine character is that He is now as He has always been, and He will forever remain as He is now. Since there is nothing about God's character that needs improvement, there is no need for Him to change—*ever*. He does not need to be kinder, gentler, nicer or more loving in any way. It is precisely because God has no sin nature that He does not need to improve His character.

Perhaps the most blessed hope of all for me is that when God gives me my new body fit for His eternal Kingdom, He will take away my sin nature. This does not mean that I (or we as citizens of His Kingdom) will then be equal to God. As His created beings, we can *never* be equal to Him due to that fact alone. It simply means that we won't have to struggle against our sin nature any longer. I can hardly wait for the time when I will no longer sin against God and against my fellow human beings. Never again will I fail to live as God intends for me or fail to show my gratitude. Never again will I speak an unkind word to my neighbor or focus solely on my own desires. Furthermore, I won't be hurt anymore by my family and friends because they were solely focused on *their* own desires. What a glorious and heavenly existence it will be!

Not only is it unnecessary for God to change, but it is *impossible* for Him to change, since He is already the epitome of flawless, sinless perfection. This means that we can expect and depend on the fact that God will always and forever be the loving, kind and gracious Father that He has always been. This characteristic of God's divine nature may well be the most joyful of all, because He is precisely the way He is.

In recent years, after I gained this understanding of God, I have found myself praying with all the worshipful gratitude I can muster how wonderful it is that God, the Father, is God and not another. Can you imagine how awful it would be if the God of all things had a different character, if He was not the loving, kind, gentle and gracious God that He is? I can tell you this one thing for certain: if that was the case, *none* of us would exist as we do right now. Any other omnipotent God would never have given us the option to reject Him. We would simply be mindless, obedient slaves to His every desire. Thank God that the One True God truly *is* God!

There are many, many more characteristics of God which I could describe for you here, but these are the basics upon which I will expound and/or refer throughout the remainder of this book. Knowing and understanding these attributes of God will enable you to truly appreciate the Salvation of our Lord. In fact, understanding your *need* for salvation is crucial both to desiring *and* appreciating the Salvation of our Lord as well. I'll get to that in the next chapter.

CHAPTER TWO: ORIGINAL SIN AND THE PROBLEM OF SIN

Now that we have a basic understanding of the character of God, let us use that understanding to make sense of our present human condition, to understand how we got into this predicament of sin in the first place (called Original Sin by theologians), to define what sin is, and to explain the ongoing problem of sin in the world and in our own lives. Once we have dealt with these matters, we will tackle the question of what we can do about it in the next chapter.

What Is the Origin of Original Sin?

Original Sin, insofar as human beings are concerned, entered our condition when Adam and Eve chose to believe the serpent's word over God's Word and eat the forbidden fruit in the Garden of Eden (Genesis 3:1-7). From that point on, a sin nature has been both physically and spiritually passed down to us from father to child, beginning with Adam. Since it is a biological fact that we get our blood type from our biological father (and our gender, too; sorry, King Henry VIII!), we should understand that we get our sin nature from our natural father as well. The Apostle Paul explained it this way:

> For since by man came death, by Man also came the resurrection of the dead. **For as in Adam all die, even so in Christ all shall be made alive** (1 Corinthians 15:21-22; emphasis added).

Death, you see, is the result of sin, just as God warned Adam in Genesis 2:16-17. This explains why Jesus had to be born of a virgin, impregnated with and by the very Word of God, instead of a sinful human father, so that Jesus would not be tainted by the curse of original sin. This, in turn, would qualify Him to be the sinless sacrifice for *all* human sin.

Paul confirms all of this for us when he states, "For as in Adam all die, even so in Christ all shall be made alive" (1 Corinthians 15:22). Jesus, in effect, is God's "do-over" human specimen to set right what Adam did wrong and to restore what Adam lost: righteousness and human dominion. God never lost dominion, but Adam did, so God came into this world as a human being to get back what He intended for humanity to have all along.

Of course, the actual point of origin for sin was when Lucifer, the covering cherub of God, chose to rebel against God and attempt to usurp God's power and take over God's throne. This is described for us in Isaiah 14 and Ezekiel 28:1-19. Don't be confused by who these Scripture passages are initially addressed to. The King of Babylon and the Prince of Tyre do not refer to human rulers but to a single spirit principality: Satan. As the Apostle Paul writes in Ephesians 6:12, "For we wrestle not against flesh and blood, but against principalities, against powers, against the rulers of the darkness of this world, against spiritual wickedness in high places" (KJV). This spirit ruler (because of the words linking him to Eden and aspiring to dethrone God) refers to Lucifer, better known to us now as Satan. *Satan* is literally the Hebrew word for *adversary*.

As far as we can tell from what is revealed to us in the holy Scriptures, there was no such thing as sin in all God's created order until Lucifer initiated and perpetuated it. Therefore, this is when I would personally "date" the origin of Original Sin. Certainly, there may be more to the story which God has opted not to reveal to us yet, which took place long, long ago in eternity past, so I have to say that I base my assertion on the revealed and written Word of God (the Bible)—as I understand it, at least—and nothing else.

God gives us a glimpse into the reason Lucifer rebelled in Ezekiel 28:15-18. Using terms that we are more familiar with today, I would say that Lucifer first became self-enamored (or narcissistic), meaning that he fell in love with himself. This sounds strangely akin to one of the Greek mythological stories about a god named Narcissus, from which we derive our English words *narcissism* and *narcissistic* today. Narcissism is classified as a psychological disorder where someone is so self-enamored that he is continually praising and aggrandizing himself and expects that everyone else sees him as he sees himself. In all my years of counseling people as both a pastor and a military chaplain, I have encountered this phenomenon only three times. Surprisingly, two cases were in the military setting and one was in the homeless shelter where I have served as a Chaplain. Though I have met a lot of arrogant and self-centered people in both the church and the military, it truly is astounding to meet a genuine narcissist. They simply can't praise themselves enough and any negative point expressed to them about themselves is quickly dismissed by them as impossible with an air of nonchalance that will make your head spin!

At any rate, Lucifer allowed himself to fall under this severe form of self-deception that no one was more beautifully created than he, which conceived in his heart a notion of personal pride and a sense of entitlement to praise and worship that are due only to the One True God. As this notion of entitlement to praise and worship grew, we must speculate at this point that Lucifer began to plot how he might dethrone God and put himself in that place which he came to believe should be his—God's throne (compare with Isaiah 14:13-14). I think we can safely assume here that this is when Lucifer "corrupted [his] wisdom for the sake of [his] splendor" (Ezekiel 28:17).

The next thing that happened in Lucifer's heart was greed. Because of his sense of entitlement, he came to expect that everything should belong to him and come under his control. Even if he had not unseated God from the throne physically (so to speak), he had done so in his own heart. God tells us through Ezekiel that

Lucifer increased his goods with abundance of trading or merchandising and "became filled with violence, And you sinned . . ." (Ezekiel 28:16). Again, we can only speculate about what sort of violence. I personally believe it was hatred–hatred for God and everyone who worshiped God–because the Apostle John tells us that hatred of brethren is equal to murder (1 John 3:15). Jesus also said of Satan that "he was a murderer from the beginning, and does not stand in the truth, because there is no truth in him," (John 8:44). It was this seething hatred that rotted Lucifer's being, that caused him to defile his sanctuaries and to multiply iniquities (Ezekiel 28:18).

In his sermon series, *The End*, Pastor Robert Morris of Gateway Church in Dallas-Fort Worth, Texas, has said, "The tough question is not, 'Why would a loving God send anyone to Hell.' No, the really tough question to answer is, 'Why would *anyone* reject a loving God?'"4 Rev. Morris calls Lucifer's attempt to dethrone God "the inexcusable rebellious rejection of God," because God had never done anything to give Lucifer and the other angels who joined in this rebellion any cause to rebel against and reject Him from being God and King over them. The same is true of Adam and Eve. They never had anything but a peaceful and loving relationship with God, until Satan (embodied in the serpent) beguiled them (Genesis 3:1-7).

So, why didn't God just destroy Satan immediately? This is a good question, and it is best answered from an understanding of God's character. This is the reason I began this book with that discussion, because we will be referring to the character of God throughout this book to respond to questions like this. It is because God is love, is righteous, is full of grace, mercy and truth, and because He is slow to anger that He is dealing with this rebellion as He is. Furthermore, God wants everyone else in His creation to understand why Satan, and those who follow his example, deserve this kind of punishment. This truth will ultimately be displayed in the end.

The fact is that God *is* going to punish Satan, but there is a due course that He must follow before that judgment will finally be carried out. It's a little like the American judicial system. When a criminal commits a crime, he or she is first arrested for suspicion of having committed the crime. Next, the crime is investigated and evidence for its perpetration is gathered. Many times, the accused may be released on a bail bond while awaiting trial. Finally, the suspect is tried in a court of law using the collected evidence. If convicted of the crime, the criminal is then sentenced and held until the judgment is carried out. We call this "due process."

In the case against Satan, God has already presented the evidence and tried, convicted and sentenced him to eternal punishment in the Lake of Fire, and he *will* be thrown into that lake at the time God has appointed. Satan is literally awaiting execution as we speak, though he is allowed the freedom to roam about the earth and continue to exercise his own will to a limited degree. All the additional crimes he has committed against

God's Law while awaiting his execution will be judged at the end of the millennial reign of Christ.

In the meantime, because God is using Satan and his cohort of demonic forces to separate those who will believe, obey, and trust in God's Word from those who will not, Satan and his evil forces are permitted to continue their exploits (with restrictions) until the appointed time. Satan and his demonic followers are all fully aware of this appointed time, though they don't know precisely when it will occur any more than we do. Nevertheless, they can know when the time is near by observing the same signs God has revealed to us in the Bible, which is why God tells us through John the Apostle in the book of Revelation:

> Then I heard a loud voice saying in heaven, "Now salvation, and strength, and the kingdom of our God, and the power of His Christ have come, for the accuser of our brethren, who accused them before our God day and night, has been cast down. And they overcame him by the blood of the Lamb and by the word of their testimony, and they did not love their lives to the death. Therefore rejoice, O heavens, and you who dwell in them! Woe to the inhabitants of the earth and the sea! **For the devil has come down to you, having great wrath, because he knows that he has a short time**" (Revelation 12:10-12; emphasis added).

There will be woe on the earth, not because Satan is a loose criminal running amuck and wreaking havoc wherever and however he chooses, but because he will further deceive those who have already rejected God and His Word, as well as some who haven't decided yet, and provoke *them* to commit deeds of wickedness and destruction, more so than ever before. This is a mistake that most people make, including many professing Christians. They give Satan far too much power and credit, if they believe in his existence at all. Satan is not an equal opposite to God doing whatever he pleases whenever he pleases. If that was true, life in this world would be a whole lot worse; believe me! No, Satan is under the authority and complete control of Almighty God, as I personally believe he has *always* been, and God has him on an ever-shortening, ever-tightening leash.

Even in the Old Testament Scriptures, during the time when some theologians assert that Satan was "out of control" until Jesus came to regain control, Satan had to have God's permission even to touch Job or anything belonging to Job (see Job chapters 1 and 2). Furthermore, even Job recognized that adversity comes with God's permission (i.e., it is sometimes permitted and other times initiated by God; it is sometimes to test and other times to judge and punish evildoing). We learn this from his response to his wife's suggestion that he should curse God so that God would take his life and get him out of his misery.

> Then his wife said to him, "Do you still hold fast to your integrity? Curse God and die!" But he said to her, "You speak as one of the foolish women speaks. **Shall we indeed accept good from God, and shall we not accept adversity?**" In all this Job did not sin with his lips (Job 2:9-10; emphasis added).

Although it was Satan who was causing the evil to befall Job, it was God who was permitting it for a purpose: to demonstrate Job's righteousness and loyalty to God and His Word (Job 1:1 &

6-8). While Satan was all too willing to attack Job, he was restricted in what he could do (Job 1:12 & 2:6). He was, in effect, a tool which God was using to further purify Job and to show us an example of how God works in *our* lives, too.

As referenced earlier in Revelation 12:10, Satan is "the accuser of our brethren," and he provokes God against us at times, either to prove our righteousness (as in Job's case; Job 2:3) or to punish our wrongdoing. God therefore uses Satan, sometimes to punish (chasten, discipline or correct, as in Hebrews 12:5-11) and sometimes to test our faith, thereby strengthening our spiritual defenses, but make no mistake: Satan is *never* out of God's strict and complete control.

Sin Defined

Most people have a pretty good idea of what sin is and what it means, but there are always some who either want to be coy or who are simply misled. Even those who want to be coy may discover after reading the ensuing pages that they don't know what they thought they knew about sin and its meaning, and those who are misled certainly need to be enlightened, too.

Rather than use Webster's dictionary for this definition, however, I will use God's definition straight out of the Bible from multiple references. There are at least four different definitions of sin found in the Bible. The first is perhaps the most straightforward definition, and it is found in 1 John 5:17. It simply states, "All unrighteousness is sin. . . ." What is unrighteousness? It is anything which contradicts or opposes what God says is right in His Word.

The second biblical definition of sin is found in James 4:17, which states, "Therefore, to him who knows to do good and does not do *it,* to him it is sin." In other words, when you know what the right thing to do is, and you choose not to do it, you've committed sin. Some have taken to distinguishing between a sin of *omission* (failing to do what is commanded) and a sin of *commission* (violating what *is* commanded), but whether you do something you *aren't* supposed to do or whether you *don't* do something you *are* supposed to do, it's still sin, just the same.

A third biblical definition of sin is found in 1 John 3:4, which states, "Whoever commits sin also commits lawlessness, and sin is lawlessness." Lawlessness literally means "living without law," but it can also mean "acting as if there is no law." We use this word today to describe someone who breaks the law without regard and/or repeatedly, as if the law doesn't exist or simply doesn't apply to him or her. That's essentially what it means here in the Scripture, too.

The final definition of sin I will use is found in Romans 14:22-23, which states,

> Do you have faith? Have *it* to yourself before God. Happy *is* he who does not condemn himself in what he approves. But he who doubts is condemned if he eats, because *he does* not *eat* from faith; for **whatever *is* not from faith is sin** (emphasis added).

This definition is a bit more complicated to explain, because the Apostle Paul is speaking about consuming meat or drink that is not kosher, either because it was sacrificed to idols or because it violates the dietary restrictions given by Moses to the people of Israel. Paul is writing to both Jews and non-Jews who now worship the Messiah together, and he explains that, because non-Jews were never required by God to abide by these dietary restrictions, and because Jesus' crucifixion was the final sacrifice which has now broken down the division between Jews and non-Jews, it is okay for Jews to partake of these foods now, since Jesus has fully satisfied the entire Law of God.

However, Paul further explains that if one is still doubtful whether he may partake of these foods (due to a lifetime of indoctrination) and does so anyway, his heart will condemn him and it will become sin for him. In this case, consuming non-kosher meat or drink without a strong personal faith that it is acceptable for him would be committing sin. Moreover, even if *you* are convinced in faith that it is okay to partake, if a brother or sister who feels that it *isn't* okay to partake challenges you about it, Paul says you should not partake, for the sake of your brother or sister who is weaker in faith, so as not to cause him or her to sin by going along with you, despite having personal reservations.

Perhaps another definition of sin which is based upon Scriptural usage, though not specifically worded in the Bible's text as the previous four I've given here, is the use of the words *offence* and *miss*. In both the Hebrew and Greek manuscripts of the Bible, the

Hebrew and Greek words translated as *sin* literally mean "an offence" or "to miss the mark." The Hebrew word used is *chatta'ah* (pronounced cot-tah-AH, Strong's H2403, חטאה)[5] and the Greek word used is *hamartia* (pronounced ham-ar-TEE-ah, Strong's G266, ἁμαρτία).[6] Therefore, when you violate God's commands in His Word, you not only miss the mark, but you also offend God.

In principle, this is no different than offending a friend or relative by saying or doing something that hurts their feelings. If you truly love them, you'll strive not to repeat those hurtful words or actions. It's no different with God. In fact, Jesus actually said, "If you love Me, keep My commandments, . . ." (John 14:15).

The Problem of Sin

The problem *of* sin is the problem *with* sin. The problem *with* sin is that it violates more than God's law; it violates God's character, hinders His perfect peace, and ultimately breaks His heart. Nevertheless, the very fact that sin exists presents an entirely new set of questions for us to consider.

Considering God's omniscience, could the problem of sin have been avoided? Through His omniscience, surely, God saw it coming. He knew that when He created Lucifer and all the other angels who later joined Lucifer in his rebellion that Lucifer would one day lead a rebellion against Him, taking one-third of the host of Heaven with him (represented by the stars in Revelation 12:3-4). So, why did God create all of them whom He knew would eventually rebel against Him? Why didn't He just leave them non-existent and avoid the painful heartache of enduring the introduction of sin into His creation? Since He knew what was coming and created these future enemies anyway, did God *intentionally* create them as evil?

Even though (in His omniscience) God surely saw it coming, considering His omnipotence, once sin was introduced into His creation, why didn't He simply use His limitless power to eradicate it immediately, restore the perfect peace and mend His wounded heart by putting the whole sordid ordeal behind Him? Why did He permit Lucifer, now renamed Satan, and all Satan's angelic followers, now called demons, to continue to spread their cancerous evil? Does this also indicate that He intentionally created them *as* evil *for* evil? How do we make sense of all this?

I will begin by answering what I deem to be the easiest question: did God *intentionally* create His future enemies as evil? The answer to that question is an emphatic "No!" God is not evil, so He would not create anything evil. However, if God *had* created them as evil, they would never have had a part in His Kingdom from the start, because God doesn't tolerate evil in His Heavenly Kingdom. The Scripture tells us,

> Let no one say when he is tempted, "I am tempted by God"; for **God cannot be tempted by evil, nor does He Himself tempt anyone** (James 1:13; emphasis added).

There is no evil in God's character. Therefore, it would be entirely against God's character and divine nature to create anything evil.

So, how did God end up with enemies, when He Himself is pure goodness and righteousness and never did anything to cause a personal rejection of His rule? The answer to that is found in one word: **choice**. I'll discuss that some more in a moment.

The answer to why God created beings which He knew would one day reject Him and introduce sin into His creation is actually quite simple. Being omnipotent, God could very easily have created beings that would never disobey His Word, but being omniscient, God knew that they wouldn't be serving Him by choice, but by His creative design.

If we try to imagine ourselves in God's place, we might suppose it would be fabulous to have beings surround and shower us with adoration and praise, eager to fulfill our every desire, until we consider that they wouldn't be doing so out of *genuine* love and desire, but because we had *made* them do so. The thrill quickly fades once we comprehend that they don't love, honor, adore, praise and serve us out of their own heart's desire, but because of our power over them. Where's the joy or pleasure in *that*?

This is precisely the situation God faced before He created the angelic host. Again, being omniscient, God knew how many angels would reject Him and how many would continue loving and serving Him, and He also knew exactly how many angels He would have to create so that He would have more who chose to remain with Him than would choose to reject Him. Therefore, He created enough to have twice as many remain with Him as would ultimately reject Him.

Many years ago, when I was a teenager, I recall some local Bible College students (who happened to attend my church) telling me that angels did not have a free will as we humans have. I accepted it then because of their status as Bible College students, but in the intervening years, I have come to reject that understanding, because they *couldn't* have rebelled if they didn't have a free will. That's the only position that makes sense.

There's still more to the story, of course, because God knew all along of His plan to create yet another order of being that would be in His own image and second in command only to Himself. God wanted this new human being who, of all His created beings, would be in His own likeness and co-ruler with Him, to have a free will to choose or reject Him. Therefore, God permitted Satan and his demons to remain on the loose, so to speak, until an appointed time. Thus, the reason God didn't leave them all nonexistent is because of His master plan to create a being in His own image with a free will to choose or reject Him as God and King. God intended all along to allow Satan to challenge His Word with Adam and Eve so that they could choose for themselves whether to believe God's Word or Satan's word.

The power of choice is very powerful indeed, and with this power comes awesome responsibility. God wanted this new order of human beings, who He would create in His own likeness for holy fellowship and co-rule, to be able to choose or reject this relationship. God was (and is), in effect, preparing an eternal companion (the Church, whom He refers to as His Bride) with whom

He will enjoy fellowship on a very intimate level. He certainly knew (because He is omniscient) that Adam and Eve would sin (violate His Word), but it was a carefully calculated decision to allow this, since the result would be worth the joy of having this eternal companion with whom to fellowship on such an intimate level ever after. While it is terribly tragic that sin must be part of the equation, God through Jesus has deemed it worth the pain and suffering so that He could obtain the joy of this everlasting intimacy with His beloved Bride (see Hebrews 12:2).

Perhaps we could understand the situation a little better if we put it in this light: sin may be compared to a grain of sand that seeps uninvited and unintended into an oyster's shell. It is a terrible, painful irritant to the oyster, but the reaction of secretion from the oyster to coat the grain as a way of coping with the pain and suffering results in a magnificent pearl that is beautiful beyond comparison and so rare to find as a natural occurrence that its value is quite high.

Because of this rarity, Jesus has compared the Kingdom of Heaven to it in Matthew 13:44-45, and God has formed the twelve gates (entrances) into the New Jerusalem City "of one pearl" (Revelation 21:21). As rare and highly valuable as just one small pearl from only one oyster is, can you estimate the value of an enormous gate made "of one pearl," let alone *twelve* of them? This demonstrates for us how highly God values the entrance into this stunning city, which an angel also calls "the bride, the Lamb's wife" (Revelation 21:9). But wait a minute–isn't the *Church* supposed to be the Bride of Christ? Where do we get that idea, and why is the New Jerusalem being called the Bride of Christ?

Although the Scripture never *specifically* calls the Church the Bride of Christ, it is implied in multiple places. The four most prominent are found in the New Testament. The first is in John 3:29, where John the Baptist says of Jesus, "He who has the bride is the bridegroom. . . ." Next, when John the Baptist's disciples asked Jesus why His disciples did not fast, Jesus replied,

> "Can the friends of the bridegroom mourn as long as the bridegroom is with them? But the days will come when the bridegroom will be taken away from them, and then they will fast" (Matthew 9:15).

Then in Paul's letters to Corinth and Ephesus, he writes:

> For I am jealous for you with godly jealousy. For I have betrothed you to one husband, that I may present *you as* a chaste virgin to Christ (2 Corinthians 11:2).

> Husbands, love your wives, just as Christ also loved the church and gave Himself for her, that He might sanctify and cleanse her with the washing of water by the word, that He might present her to Himself a glorious church, not having spot or wrinkle or any such thing, but that she should be holy and without blemish. So husbands ought to love their own wives as their own bodies; he who loves his wife loves himself. For no one ever hated his own flesh, but nourishes and cherishes it, just as the Lord *does* the church. **For we are members of His body, of His flesh and of His bones. "FOR THIS REASON A MAN SHALL LEAVE HIS FATHER AND MOTHER AND BE JOINED TO HIS WIFE, AND THE TWO SHALL BECOME ONE FLESH." This is a great mystery, but I speak concerning**

Christ and the church (Ephesians 5:25-32; emphasis added).

Paul's reference to the church not having spot or wrinkle is also faintly like a short passage in the Song of Solomon. It states, "You *are* all fair, my love, And *there is* no spot in you" (Song of Solomon 4:7). Most Bible scholars agree that the purpose of including the Song of Solomon in the body of Scripture, though it is a literal story of Solomon and his Shulamite Bride, is because of its metaphorical comparison to the passionate love shared between God and His people (both Israel and the Church). I, too, agree with this interpretation.

To answer the question of why both the Church and the New Jerusalem are referred to as the Bride of Christ, I believe it is much the same as when we refer to the church today. We say we're going *to church*, and yet we say that *the people are the church*. So, which is it? Just as we call the building where we meet for worship *the church*, and just as we call the worship service *going to church* or *having church*, and just as we call the people who make up the congregation of believers in Jesus Christ *the church*, both the New Jerusalem (the place where the people of God will dwell *with* God forever) and the people themselves constitute *the Church*, the Bride of Christ. Therefore, both the people of God and the place where they will live with God forever are *the Bride of Christ*.

The problem of sin and the problem *with* sin is a constant irritant in the lives of true (i.e., sincere) believers in Jesus Christ. If there had been a better way for God to acquire this eternal, intimate relationship (fellowship) with His beloved people, He most certainly would have chosen it. Even Jesus prayed in the Garden of Gethsemane, ". . . O My Father, if it is possible, let this cup pass from Me; nevertheless, not as I will, but as You *will*." (Matthew 26:39). He was asking if there was any other way to accomplish the divine goal of intimate union with His beloved human creation without going to the cross and to Hell. **We can surmise from the fact that God sent Jesus to the cross to suffer and die *anyway* as proof that there was no other way possible.**

Our present condition *is* the best option available to God and to us. The truly Good News is that God has made a provision for overcoming this terrible set of circumstances, both for Him and us. None of us has to be lost to Him forever if we will only accept the Plan of Salvation He has laid out for us and follow His instructions for obtaining that salvation. It really does come down to a matter of acceptance and trust in what God has said and done. Will you accept the Word of God and put your trust in His Plan of Salvation, His Savior for us, Jesus Christ?

The power of choice is indeed powerful, and we are fully responsible for the choice we make. However, God has done everything necessary to save us, including giving us the right choice to make. As He said through Moses,

> I call heaven and earth as witnesses today against you,
> *that* I have set before you life and death, blessing and
> cursing; therefore **choose life**, that both you and your

descendants may live. . . (Deuteronomy 30:19; emphasis added).

Truly, God has made the provision, but we must make the decision. All we must do is decide.

In the next chapter, we'll look at what to do about our sin condition and how to cope with it until that glorious day when Christ returns for us. Are you ready for His return? He's coming sooner than anyone thinks!

CHAPTER THREE: MUCH ADO ABOUT WHAT TO DO

Having explained the origin and the problem of sin, as well as giving the biblical definition of sin, let us now proceed to deal with what to do about the ongoing problem of sin in our lives. If we are born with original sin through no fault of our own, why does God hold us responsible for our sins? If we must take personal responsibility for our sins, how do we continue to live our lives for Christ with this problem of sin? Furthermore, if God is righteous and demands *us* to be righteous so that we can have divine fellowship with Him, how will we ever be able to attain this? These are all excellent questions, so let's answer each one in turn now.

Whose Fault Is It, Anyway?

If you need someone to blame for the introduction and existence of sin in the world, look no further than Satan. However, too many Christians turn this fact into a presupposed excuse for sin.

During the 1970s, Flip Wilson was a popular comedian with his own television show. On this show, he used to do a comedy routine where he dressed up like a woman that he dubbed Geraldine and prated about all the things she had done wrong. Her justification for each one was consistently, "The Devil made me do it!" While his goofy costume and smug self-justification routine drew a lot of laughs, it depicts even now the degree to which many Christians (not to mention non-Christians) have attempted to relinquish personal responsibility for their sins.

Just as Satan had the power to choose whether to rebel or continue honoring and obeying God, so every human being has the power to choose between rebellion against God and obedience to Him. The problem for us humans, though, is that once our forebear Adam sinned, the genetic make-up of his seed was tainted by sin. (Literally, the word *sperma* is Greek[7] and the word *semen* is Latin[8] for *seed*.) Consequently, when Adam fathered children, he set in motion the perpetual curse of sin which was then passed from generation to generation from father to child, even until now. So, why didn't God simply sterilize Adam to prevent this from happening? Well, aside from the fact that God had already commanded Adam and Eve to be fruitful and multiply, it was also because this father-to-child transmission of sin was part of God's grand design, since He knew from the start that He would need a way to interject Himself into His own creation and set right what He knew would go wrong once Adam sinned.

Therefore, as much as we may desire to pass the blame and escape personal responsibility for our sin, we cannot, because

God will not excuse us apart from His plan. Sin is a part of humanity's fallen nature. Therefore, we call it our *sin nature*. While we have no choice over the problem of being born with sin, and although it seems we cannot indefinitely resist the temptation to commit sin (even after yielding our soul to Christ's Lordship), we are ultimately and personally responsible for every sin we commit, even after choosing to follow Jesus Christ.

There's a great deal of misunderstanding and misinformation being taught in the church today about our responsibility for sin after we accept Jesus as our personal Lord and Savior. Many are teaching that once we accept Christ as our Savior, we are *in* Christ (as the Apostle Paul says repeatedly throughout his epistles) and therefore righteous because *Jesus* is righteous. Thus, we are no longer held responsible for our sins committed after accepting Christ. This is simply not true! Let me explain.

Being in Christ means receiving and having a part in His Plan of Salvation and being in continual relationship with Him. It does *not* mean *becoming* or *blending into* Christ. Despite being called the *Body of Christ* (1 Corinthians 12:27) and *becoming one with* Christ (John 17:20-23), we are *not Christ*. The unity of the Church (and the union of the Church with Christ) will not occur until sometime after the Rapture of the Church and the Marriage Supper of the Lamb (Revelation 19:7-9), at the earliest.

Although we will receive a new sinless body at the Rapture (i.e., at the time of our resurrection), until then we continue to live in the same body we had *before* we accepted God's Plan of

Salvation, so we continue to be tempted to commit sin. In fact, whereas before we accepted Christ we rarely wrestled with our conscience over our sin (though perhaps we did feel guilty on occasion), *after* we accept Christ, we are called to *resist* the temptation to sin, and we find that we now wrestle against yielding to the temptation to commit sin *daily*! The Apostle Paul describes this terrific tension between resisting and committing sin quite well in his letter to the Romans.

> For what I am doing, I do not understand. For what I will to do, that I do not practice; but what I hate, that I do. . . . For the good that I will *to do,* I do not do; but the evil I will not *to do,* that I practice (Romans 7:15 & 19).

This is the problem we *all* have with sin and our sin nature! Paul continues to explain that, since he does not desire to break God's law, he is basically being pressed to do so by the law of sin that rules over his flesh (Romans 7:23).

Now, for those who conclude after reading this that we are therefore not responsible for our sins, they are missing the point entirely. We are called by Christ to come *out* of our sinful lifestyle and begin living a life of righteousness for Jesus' sake. How is it for Jesus' sake, and what is a "life of righteousness"? It is for Jesus' sake because He bore the punishment for all our sins when He died on the cross and descended into "the lower parts of the earth" (Hell), as Paul wrote about in Ephesians 4:9. Also, Jesus Himself said regarding His death,

> For as Jonah was three days and three nights in the belly
> of the great fish, so will the Son of Man be three days and
> three nights **in the heart of the earth** (Matthew 12:40;
> see also Jonah 1:17; emphasis added).

You see then that Jesus was sweating "great drops of blood" (Luke 22:24) for more than the physical suffering He would have to endure leading up to and on the cross. He was recoiling (Matthew 26:36-42) from the imposition of sin and the punishment of Hell that He would endure for us as well (2 Corinthians 5:21 and Ephesians 4:9).

We truly have no idea how much Jesus suffered for us so that He could provide a way of salvation whereby we might escape the punishment of Hell. Therefore, rather than delighting in sin and treating it so lightly, we should push ourselves to the point of sweating "great drops of blood" to *avoid* sinning as much as we can. We should remind ourselves that for every sin we commit in thought, word or deed, it was heaped upon Jesus' shoulders, and He bore the punishment for it not only on the cross, but in Hell itself.

So, what is living a life of righteousness? That is a very simple and easy question to answer. Righteous living is practicing a lifestyle filled with thoughts, words, and deeds that conform to the Holy Word of God. What is the Word of God? It is contained in the book we know as *The Holy Bible*. Read and obey the commands in that book as much as you can, and you will live a life of righteousness. However, because none of us can live a life that is totally righteous, we need someone who *can* live in total righteousness to absorb the punishment for our sins. His name is Jesus.

Okay, now that we understand that we are personally responsible for our sins, and that God *will* hold us accountable for every one of them (see 2 Corinthians 5:10), how do we live a life of righteousness when faced with this daily obstacle of sin? Do we just throw our hands up in surrender because it's so hard? Let's talk about that.

How to Live for Christ with Our Sin Nature

I believe people who identify themselves as Christian today fall into one of four categories. They are either living in despondency and defeat over their inability to avoid committing sin (because they deeply desire to be righteous and holy before God) or they are living in licentiousness, claiming they are "under grace" and "not under law" (Romans 6:14), or they are misguided by the thinking that they are Christian by association (i.e., because their parents are Christian or their father is/was a pastor or because they attend religious services, etc.). The fourth and final category is for those who truly have a right understanding of the Scriptures regarding their relationship with Jesus Christ, and they live their lives accordingly. There's really no need to discuss this fourth category, since those Christians are already successful at living for Christ with their sin nature, except to say that they are in the minority. However, I will briefly touch on each of the other three categories to explain how to move from one of these other three into the fourth category.

If you're besieged with self-loathing, despondency, and personal defeat over your inability to avoid committing sins in your Christian life, you're allowing your thinking to be influenced by demonic forces. The Scripture tells us that Satan is "the accuser of our brethren" (Revelation 12:10) and that he (or his demonic cohorts) will frequently remind us of our sins, both past and present. You are going to have to consider and decide whether you're going to accept and believe God's Word, that upon our confession and repentance He will remove our sins from us "as far as the east is from the west" (Psalm 103:12), or whether you will believe Satan's word that God is still holding them against you. If you want to be truly free from your guilt and shame, you must read, accept, and believe (that means *trust* in) what God's Word says in the Bible.

On the other hand, if you think you must demonstrate ongoing remorse through self-flagellation (in either a physical or a figurative sense) to prove your humility and penitence for your sin, you may be caught up in a form of spiritual pride, thinking you are somehow paying for your sins (the theological term is *atonement*). The same is true if you think you can perform any other sort of ritual, such as saying the Lord's Prayer a certain number of times or making a sizable donation to the local church or some other charitable organization. Not only is it impossible for any of us to pay for even *one* of our sins (which is why Jesus came into the world and died on the cross in the first place), but it is an affront to Jesus and His atoning work on the cross for us to even *attempt* such a thing!

If you're among those who feel despondent and defeated because you're incapable of living without sin, you're almost there. Now that you've recognized the reality, take a deep breath, turn to Jesus, and put your total trust in *His* perfect sinlessness as your only hope of being righteous before God. Believe that Jesus exchanged *His* righteousness for *your* sins when He died in your place on the cross. Accept God's forgiveness and His promise to give you an everlasting life with Him for believing that. The next time you feel defeated by your sin nature, remind yourself of God's Holy Word, which says,

> For by grace you have been saved through faith, and that not of yourselves; *it is* **the gift of God, not of works, lest anyone should boast** (Ephesians 2:8-9; emphasis added).

Okay, that's one extreme, where someone feels helpless and hopeless to live a godly Christian life with our sin nature. Now, let's consider the other extreme, where someone feels empowered to completely ignore God's Word (His commandments to live righteously, at least) and chooses to live an unrestrained lifestyle because Jesus has "paid it all, all to Him I owe"[9] and because we Christians live "under grace" rather than "under law" (Romans 6:14). This attitude is just as wrong and just as dangerous to the soul as the first category described above. I call this the licentious Christian, though I hesitate to tag such a person as Christian at all. Certainly, it is up to God to decide when and on whom to show His grace. As He told Moses,

> I will be gracious to whom I will be gracious, and I will have compassion on whom I will have compassion (Exodus 33:19; see also Romans 9:14-16).

Therefore, I am perfectly content to leave all the judging up to God, who is the only Righteous Judge.

If you are one who believes you don't have to obey God's Law (which is synonymous with His Word) simply because of one statement written by the Apostle Paul in Romans 6:14, go back and re-read that passage of Scripture. Here's what the entire, unabridged verse states:

> **For sin shall not have dominion over you,** for you are not under law but under grace (Romans 6:14; emphasis added).

Did you notice the first half of that sentence? Read it again. It clearly says, "For sin shall not have dominion over you. . . ." If you have thrown off restraint and hopped on board the "we live under grace not under law" bandwagon, you have given yourself over to slavery to sin. Go ahead and read the next two verses following the one just quoted above. They state:

> What then? Shall we sin because we are not under law but under grace? Certainly not! **Do you not know that to whom you present yourselves slaves to obey, you are that one's slaves whom you obey,**

whether of sin *leading* to death, or of obedience *leading* to righteousness? (Romans 6:15-16; compare with John 8:34; emphasis added).

You see, the Apostle Paul has not given *anyone* a license to sin. In fact, *license* is the root word for *licentious,* and it refers to someone who feels he has a license (permission) to sin. This is simply not true! As Paul says in the passage above, if you simply give in to sin every time you're tempted, without offering any resistance, you are *enslaving* yourself to your sin nature and ultimately to Satan, who is the father of sin. Now, if you're enslaved to Satan, how can you belong to Christ?

So, how can you avoid falling into this trap of licentiousness? It's very easy; simply devote time in your day to reading and contemplating (i.e., meditating upon) the meaning and application of God's Word, and it will stick in your heart and mind and rise to the forefront of your memory each time you're faced with temptation. Gaining understanding from God's Word is also known as *revelation.* As wise King Solomon also wrote,

> Where *there is* no revelation, the people cast off restraint;
> But happy *is* he who keeps the law (Proverbs 29:18).

Other translations word it differently, giving various alternative words for *revelation* and *restraint*, but I believe the New King James Version I've quoted here is quite accurate. The original Hebrew words for *revelation* and *restraint* are (*chazon*, pronounced *khaw-ZONE,* Strong's H2377, חזון and *para,* pronounced paw-RAH, Strong's H6544, פּרע),[10] respectively. *Chazon* means a mental sight, such as a dream, revelation, oracle or vision. *Para* means to loosen, expose or absolve. Therefore, when people have no word from the Lord (i.e., a revelation, vision, dream, or even a memorized Scripture), they will loosen their legal and moral restraints. In short, they will become lawless and licentious.

If you are one of those claiming to be a Christian while ignoring God's Word/commandments to live righteously according His standard, the surest way to rectify your error is to begin reading and applying what you understand from God's Word to how you live your life. Obedience to God's Holy Word (insofar as we are able) is the surest way to live for Christ with our sin nature. No one should deceive himself into thinking he can live a sinless life by obeying God's Word alone, however, and neither should he surrender to every temptation because it's so difficult to live without sinning every day, but when we strive to avoid sinning by doing what God's Word commands, we can trust in the wonderful, matchless grace of our Lord to forgive us when we sin. I'll write a little more about that in the next section of this chapter, so I'll hold those thoughts until then.

The third category of people who identify themselves as Christian is not genuinely Christian at all. There is no such thing as being a Christian by association. If everyone in your family is a committed believer in Jesus Christ, yet you have never made your own personal commitment to Him, you are not automatically a Christian simply because your family members are Christians, nor does going to religious services or joining a local church make you a Christian. Someone has jokingly said, "Sitting in a church does not make one a Christian any more than standing in a garage makes one an automobile." How true that is!

So, what should you do if you were one of those misguided people until just now? The answer to that question is very easy. Simply acknowledge that you must have your own personal relationship with Jesus Christ before you can rest assured of having eternal life with Him in His coming Kingdom. You then must confess your need for forgiveness of your sins and cease living a lifestyle that dismisses the will of God for you and begin striving to obey God's Word and live a life of righteousness for Him. If you do these things by faith (i.e., by trusting that He will keep His promise, His Word to you), then God will grant you His salvation. It's just that simple!

Now, once we understand that we are to live our lives for Christ's sake, despite having to wrestle with our sin nature every day, we will next discuss how to maintain this fellowship with Christ. Let's look at that now.

How to Maintain Fellowship with Christ

Aside from the erroneous notion that once we accept Christ we are no longer responsible for our sins, these same aforementioned misguided teachers (some may actually be *intentionally false* teachers) are teaching that we don't need to confess or repent from the sins we commit after accepting

Christ because all of our sins–past, present, and future–were covered by the blood of Jesus. While they are partly correct– the blood of Jesus does indeed cover all our sins, past, present, and future–we must still confess and repent of these sins to maintain holy fellowship with Christ. The Apostle Paul wrote it this way:

> For *it is* not possible that the blood of bulls and goats could take away sins. Therefore, when He [Jesus Christ] came into the world, He said: "SACRIFICE AND OFFERING YOU DID NOT DESIRE, BUT A BODY YOU HAVE PREPARED FOR ME. IN BURNT OFFERINGS AND SACRIFICES FOR SIN YOU HAD NO PLEASURE. THEN I SAID, 'BEHOLD, I HAVE COME– IN THE VOLUME OF THE BOOK IT IS WRITTEN OF ME– TO DO YOUR WILL, O GOD.'" Previously saying, "SACRIFICE AND OFFERING, BURNT OFFERINGS, AND OFFERINGS FOR SIN YOU DID NOT DESIRE, NOR HAD PLEASURE IN THEM" (which are offered according to the law), then He said, "BEHOLD, I HAVE COME TO DO YOUR WILL, O GOD." He takes away the first that He may establish the second. By that will we have been sanctified through the offering of the body of Jesus Christ once *for all*. And every priest stands ministering daily and offering repeatedly the same sacrifices, which can never take away sins. But this Man [Jesus], after He had offered one sacrifice for sins forever, sat down at the right hand of God. . . (Hebrews 10:4-12).

Where I think these other teachers are mistaken in their interpretation and understanding is that although Jesus' sacrifice for our sins was once and for all, forever, we must still apply His atoning blood each time we commit sin after we receive His salvation, not because we must be saved all over again, but so we can restore our fellowship with Him, which is broken each time we sin. This is akin to the way God's people of the Old Covenant brought sin offerings, not to become God's people all over again, but to restore their fellowship with God. I base this conclusion on the final two verses quoted above. Paul stated:

> And every priest stands ministering daily and offering repeatedly the same sacrifices, which can never take away sins. But this Man, after He had offered one sacrifice for sins forever, sat down at the right hand of God. . . (Hebrews 10:11-12).

The fact that these former priests offered their sacrifices repeatedly means that the sacrifices were offered after each confession of sin by the one bringing the sacrifice. However, whereas the blood of bulls and goats could not take away sins (Hebrews 10:4 & 11), Jesus' perfect, sinless blood is sufficient to be applied repeatedly after only one offering—for all and forevermore. Therefore, His blood is applied first for cleansing and purging from all our sins until the moment when we accept His atoning Plan of Salvation. Then it is reapplied repeatedly throughout the remainder of our lives to restore our fellowship with Him each time we break that fellowship with sin. Jesus' sacrifice was sufficient for every human sin that has ever been committed, and that ever *will be* committed, until the end of the final age on this present earth.

Hitler's sins of murdering six million Jews, plus millions of others, among his other lesser-known sins of blasphemy, lying, etc., were all covered by the blood of Jesus, except Hitler apparently chose not to accept Jesus' atonement for his sins. Stalin's sins of murdering 20 million or more of his own people out of paranoia were covered by the blood of Jesus, except he also apparently chose not to accept Jesus' atonement for his sins. I could name many other famous sinners who chose not to accept Jesus' atonement for their sins, but I think you get the point. Jesus' blood sacrifice was sufficient for *all* these horrible sins. What's more, to make it personal, Jesus' blood is sufficient to cover *my* sins and *your* sins, too.

So, if Jesus' blood sacrifice is sufficient for all our sins—past, present and future—how exactly do we maintain fellowship with Him, since we are so prone to commit sin, even after accepting Him as our Savior? First of all, we must walk humbly with Him (Micah 6:8), never thinking more highly of ourselves than we ought to think (Romans 12:3), and confess our sins whenever the Holy Spirit brings them to our attention (1 John 1:9). As the Apostle John wrote:

> This is the message which we have heard from Him and declare to you, that God is light and in Him is no darkness at all. If we say that we have fellowship with Him, and walk in darkness, we lie and do not practice the truth. But if we walk in the light as He is in the light, we have fellowship with one another, and the blood of Jesus Christ His Son cleanses us from all sin. **If we say that we have no sin, we deceive ourselves, and the truth is not in us. If we confess our sins, He is faithful and just to forgive us *our* sins and to cleanse us from all unrighteousness. If we say that we have not sinned, we make Him a liar, and His word is not in us** (1 John 1:5-10; emphasis added).

In other words, since John is writing to believers in the Church, not to unbelievers, as one of these other misguided teachers has taught, we are to understand that we cannot claim to be in fellowship with Christ if we are practicing sin. Now, there's a big difference between someone who commits an *occasional* sin (because he is striving to live righteously and obediently before the Lord) and someone who is living a *lifestyle* of sin, which is *practicing* sin. Even though the one who commits an occasional sin must still confess and repent of that specific violation of God's Word to restore his fellowship with Christ, this one who claims to be in fellowship with Christ, yet practices sin without restraint and does not confess and repent of this lifestyle of sin, is living in self-deceit. John tells us that such a one does "not practice the truth" (1 John 1:6).

If you dare ask the question that Pilate asked Jesus at His trial, "What is truth?" (John 18:38), you will display the same ignorance that Pilate did. While Pilate thought it was a rhetorical question and did not wait for Jesus to give him an answer, Jesus had already answered that question for His disciples and for us the night before. In His *real* Lord's Prayer, a personal prayer Jesus offered to God the Father on behalf of His disciples on the night of His arrest, He prayed, "Sanctify them by Your truth. **Your word is truth**" (John 17:17; emphasis added).

If God's Word is truth, then we are to judge all supposed truth by the standard of God's Word. Therefore, any statement which contradicts God's Word on *any* point is most assuredly *not* the truth. Furthermore, anyone who tries to add to or take away from

84

God's Word is to be summarily dismissed and ignored. Indeed, such a one is in great danger spiritually (see Revelation 22:18-19)!

Maintaining fellowship with Christ is best done by focusing on God's Word. So long as we seek to spend as much time as possible mining for gems of wisdom and revelation from God's Word, we won't be disappointed, and we will grow ever stronger in our faith *in* Him, in our knowledge *of* Him, and in our love and devotion *for* Him. We will find ourselves being drawn ever deeper into this truly holy fellowship that we are privileged to have with Him. What a magnificent process and experience it is!

Now, having settled the question of how to live with our sin nature, let us move on to searching out the facts about our Savior's origin and our dire need for Him. Like everything else in God's creation, it all started with a seed—a Seed of Promise.

CHAPTER FOUR: THE SEED OF PROMISE

Now that we have discussed the problem of sin and how to live more effectively for Christ with our original sin nature, we will proceed next to discuss God's plan to deal with the problem of sin in His human creatures once and forever. Since we learned of God's omniscience in the first chapter, we know that God foreknew everything that would happen before He ever created the world and all that is in it, including the sin of Lucifer and Lucifer's temptation of the first man and woman in the Garden of Eden to join him in the terrible throes of sin. Therefore, God proceeded anyway with creating the universe and all that is in it, including Lucifer, all the many angels, and humanity, despite knowing the outcome of their choices to sin against Him. Why did He do this? He did it because He had a plan for overcoming this temporarily disappointing outcome. As Hebrews 12:2 states,

> ". . . looking unto Jesus, the author and finisher of *our* faith, who **for the joy that was set before Him endured the cross,** despising the shame, and has

sat down at the right hand of the throne of God" (emphasis added).

So, what was God's plan, and how is it playing out right now? I'm glad you asked!

The Seed of the Woman

It all started with a mysterious prophecy from God's own mouth. It is the first of what theologians call "Messianic Prophecies." God pronounced this promise at the beginning of a series of curses He placed upon the serpent, the woman, the man, and all of creation in response to the sin which Adam and Eve had committed due to the serpent's deception and temptation. Speaking to the serpent, God said,

> "And I will put enmity Between you and the woman, And between your seed and her Seed; He shall bruise your head, And you shall bruise His heel" (Genesis 3:15).

What could this mean? How would God bring it to pass, and *when*? It was a proverbial shot across the bow of Satan's ship of state. He had no idea how or when God would fulfill His promise, but knowing God as he did, he knew that whatever God said He would do was as good as done. However, I am not sure whether Satan had deceived himself into believing he could somehow thwart God's plans and promises or if he thought he could only postpone them. By now, it should be quite clear to him that he can do neither. All the times Satan *thought* he was delaying God's plan was actually part of God's timetable after all. Being omniscient, God factored in all these attempts to thwart His plan and made them into part of the schedule. Everything has been going according to God's divine plan and schedule all along, and the culminating event of Jesus' eternal enthronement is rapidly approaching.

Since it is a biological fact that the male produces the seed and the female produces the egg, how was a woman, *any* woman, going to produce a seed that would threaten Satan's dominion by crushing his head? This was a mystery which God kept to Himself until the time of Isaiah the prophet. Isaiah was the first to prophesy:

> Therefore the Lord Himself will give you a sign: Behold, the virgin shall conceive and bear a Son, and shall call His name Immanuel (Isaiah 7:14).

Even then, it was difficult to see, since God hid this revelation in the middle of another prophecy about Syria and Ephraim who were plotting against King Ahaz of Judah. Since part of it refers to the coming Seed of Promise (see Isaiah 7:14-15) and part of it refers to Isaiah's own son in his arms (see Isaiah 7:3 & 16), this prophetic word is somewhat confusing. I must admit it had me stumped until I read Matthew Henry's commentary where he explained it quite well.[11] Nevertheless, it is the primary promise we Christians point to every Advent-Christmastide when we announce again the birth of our Savior Jesus Christ. It was partially fulfilled (the virgin conception part, at least) in Luke 1:26-35 when Gabriel announced to Mary what was about to happen to her. Further affirmation of this fulfillment is found in Matthew 1:18 & 22-23 when Matthew, under the inspiration of the Holy Spirit, quotes Isaiah 7:14 as a prophetic fulfillment at Jesus' conception and birth.

At the time God pronounced His prophetic promise in Genesis 3:15 that the woman's seed would crush the serpent's head, I'm certain neither Satan nor Eve nor Adam understood how this would play out. In fact, it appears that Eve thought this promise was about to be fulfilled with the birth of Cain:

> Now Adam knew Eve his wife, and she conceived and bore Cain, and said, **"I have acquired a man from the LORD"** (Genesis 4:1; emphasis added).

According to *Fausset's Bible Dictionary*,[12] the name Cain means "acquired," while other Bible dictionaries, including *Hitchcock's Bible Names*[13] gives "possession, or possessed" as the meaning. By saying, "I have acquired a man from the LORD," Eve seems to be saying that she believes Cain will be the one who will bruise the serpent's head. It may be that because of Eve's statement Satan feared this to be true, too. Perhaps that is why he targeted Cain and ultimately turned him against his brother Abel so that he committed the first murder by killing Abel. It seems then that every time a truly righteous man arose on the earth that Satan suspected him of being "the One" and sought to destroy him in one way or another.

Eve seems to have revised her view after Cain killed Abel. At the time of Seth's birth, we read,

> And Adam knew his wife again, and she bore a son and named him Seth, "For **God has appointed another seed for me** instead of Abel, whom Cain killed" (Genesis 4:25; emphasis added).

Don't forget that Adam and Eve had many other children besides Cain, Abel and Seth (Genesis 4:13-17 & 5:3-4), which makes Eve's words all-the-more poignant. What was in Eve's mind that distinguished Seth from all her other sons? Did God tell her or Adam something about Seth that singled him out from all the others? God simply doesn't tell us in the text.

In addition to targeting individual men, Satan also seems to have devised a broader, more sinister plan for thwarting God's planned Seed of Promise. Moreover, Satan's plan fit right in with God's prophetic word that not only would the woman produce a Seed, but Satan would produce a seed as well, and his seed would be at enmity with the woman's Seed (Genesis 3:15). This prophetic word from the Lord appears to be applicable in at least three ways.

First, Satan's seed is–because of the sin nature–already a spiritually corrupt one, but it is furthermore rejected by God because it is wholly loyal to Satan and his plan. This seed would therefore continually rival those among humanity who are spiritually regenerated and choose to live for God.

Second, this seed of Satan would also continually rival those who are called and chosen out from humanity by God to be His peculiar people. Initially, this was Abraham and his descendants (later called Israel), but it now includes people of both Hebrew and non-Hebrew descent who have accepted Jesus Christ.

Third, Satan's seed will continually rival God's holy Seed, the Messiah. Since the Messiah is the One who literally crushes his head, Satan hates Him the most and uses his seed to act as an anti-messiah (i.e., one that both opposes and attempts to replace the true Messiah). However, due to translation from Greek to English, we know this term better as "antichrist" than "anti-messiah," even though they basically mean the same. I'll get more into the meanings of these names and what's in a name in the next chapter.

So, what was Satan's plan, and just how would Satan produce a seed? His initial plan seems to have been to corrupt the seeds of humanity by seducing human women and producing a hybrid offspring called by the Hebrew term *Nephilim* (literally "fallen ones" as rendered in *Young's Literal Translation*) and translated as "giants" in the King James English Bible. This would eventually leave no pure-bred seed on the earth from which God could raise up His Seed of Promise. It appears Satan had nearly succeeded when God intervened to destroy the earth with a flood, sparing only one righteous man and his family (see Genesis 6:1-8).

Though Satan once again attempted to corrupt the human genome *after* the Flood (see Genesis 6:4), he also tried a different tact by using a man named Nimrod (grandson of Ham and great-grandson of Noah; see Genesis 10:6-8) to try to gather everyone on earth under his rule. However, God intervened again, this time by confusing everyone's single language into multiple languages, thus forcing everyone to disperse throughout the earth (see Genesis 10:8-10 & 11:1-9). Apparently, this was also the point when God set the boundaries of all the nations on earth, as described for us by the Apostle Paul in Acts 17:26.

Setting the Stage

Not long after this confusion of language and global dispersion of the people, God set in motion the next phase of His plan. It had been nearly two thousand years since Adam and Eve's sin when God had issued His first Messianic Prophecy, and now He was ready to issue His next prophecy about yet another seed of promise coming forth from a most unlikely couple named Abram and Sarai, whom God later renamed Abraham and Sarah. Not only had Sarah been infertile all her life, but she was already past childbearing age when God chose her husband and her to be the ones to bear this new promised seed who would be named Isaac, which means *laughter*. This name implies not only the humor of two aged people conceiving and giving birth to a baby but God's laughter at Satan and his minions for thinking they could outwit and overpower Him in *any* contest (compare with Psalm 2:2-4).

From Isaac would come a nation set apart for God and His divine purposes and from whom the ultimate Seed of Promise, Jesus, would also descend. Nevertheless, the arrival of this promised child (Isaac) would not take place for another 25 years after God first promised it to Abraham.

In the meantime, Sarah dreamed up a plan of her own to help fulfill God's plan. Since she knew very well that she was already past childbearing, she decided to use the customary practice of surrogacy that was widely accepted at that time and let her Egyptian handmaid, Hagar, bear the promised child unto Abraham (Genesis 16). Little did she or Abraham know the sort of trouble this decision would cause throughout the remainder of human history, even until today! The descendants of Ishmael, this son produced by Abraham and Hagar, would ultimately become Israel's greatest enemy of all time. They are none other than the Arab people, through which Satan has also raised up a false religion (called Islam) with the fully stated intent of completely eradicating Israel from the earth!

A Woman from the Seed of Promise

Before God would produce the *Seed* of the woman, however, He first needed to produce the *woman* who would produce the Seed. Who is this woman? It is none other than the nation of Israel, which God refers to on at least one occasion as His wife (Jeremiah 3:14). The fact that Israel is the woman who would bear the Seed of Promise is also revealed to us in chapter 12 of the Book of Revelation. We see from the imagery of Revelation 12 that this nation (beginning with the seed of Isaac from Father Abraham) would become the woman who would bear the Seed of

Promise (Jesus) that would ultimately destroy Satan and his kingdom forever. Furthermore, this entire redemptive story from the Bible is also told in the constellations of the stars, and the scene that is described in Revelation 12:1 seems to be the sign of Virgo (or "the Virgin") in the heavens at a particular point on the celestial clock face. However, because I do not intend to go into detail about this aspect of the stars, their constellations, and their relationship to the Bible's redemptive story, I refer you to other sources for more study on that subject, if you're interested. E. W. Bullinger's classic work, *The Witness of the Stars*, is an invaluable reference for this study.

Although Mary would be the actual virgin who would conceive and give physical birth to the Messiah, Israel is to be understood in another sense as the woman who would produce the Seed of Promise, the One who would crush Satan's head (based largely upon Revelation 12). Therefore, God set about generating her (both Israel and Mary, who would later come from Israel) by starting with an infertile couple already past the age of childbearing and giving them only one son named Isaac–Laughter.

Like a mighty oak that came from a tiny acorn, Israel grew from one baby boy to a mighty nation of millions. Not only did Isaac fulfill God's promise to Abraham and Sarah, but he also became a type (or picture) of the ultimate Seed of Promise (Jesus Christ) who would come much later. Abraham's offering of Isaac on Mount Moriah (the same location where the Temple of Solomon would later be built) bears a strong resemblance to the offering of Jesus Christ on the cross near the same location about two thousand years later, but with one obvious exception–God *went through with* the sacrifice of His Son Jesus, whereas He stopped Abraham *before* Abraham could slay Isaac on the altar (Genesis 22:10-12).

Interestingly, when Isaac married Rebekah, she, too, was infertile until Isaac prayed for God to heal her (Genesis 25:21). Perhaps her infertility was a simple test of Isaac's faith to see whether he would claim the promise which his father Abraham most certainly would have shared with him. It would be several years later, however, before God would appear to Isaac and give him this same promise in Genesis 26:1-5 & 24.

Once Rebekah became pregnant, she bore fraternal twins. During her pregnancy, God explained to her that her two sons would become two nations, that one would be stronger than the other, and that the older would serve the younger (Genesis 25:23). It appears that Satan was also aware of this information and that he used it to try to kill the younger son, Jacob (Genesis 27:41), and end God's plan for both a nation and a promised Seed. Nevertheless, God, in His omniscience and omnipotence, protected His promises during every attack of Satan.

The Promised Line

Although God dropped a few "breadcrumbs" of insightful information over the next several generations after Abraham (such as Genesis 49:10-11; Deuteronomy 18:18-19; and Numbers 24:17

& 19), it was not until the time of David, the youngest son of Jesse, that God pronounced His next poignant prophecy regarding the Seed of Promise. It was approximately one thousand years following God's last prophetic pronouncement to Abraham regarding the Seed of Promise, and approximately three thousand years following God's initial prophetic pronouncement to Satan, Adam, and Eve in the Garden of Eden, but this time, God prophesied that this Seed of Promise would come directly from the line of David, a man after God's own heart (2 Samuel 7:1-17; 13:13-14; and Acts 13:21-23).

Some years after David was established as King of Israel, he decided to build a house for God to dwell in, but God chose instead to give that privilege to David's son, Solomon, who would succeed him on the throne (2 Chronicles 28:1-7). Moreover, God promised to build a house for David which would not be a physical dwelling but a family lineage. While this prophecy contained a dual application—referring both to David's direct descendants and to the coming Seed of the woman—it could be fulfilled only by the Seed of Promise, since only the Messiah will rule forever (2 Samuel 7:16; Isaiah 9:6-7; and Daniel 2:44).

Since Mary, the mother of Jesus, descended from this Davidic line, Jesus fulfilled God's promise both to David and to Satan, Adam, and Eve all at once! It would not be until after Jesus' birth, however, that the complete line of Jesus' genealogy would reveal exactly who were the ones through whom Jesus had descended. In fact, two of the four New Testament Gospel writers, Matthew and Luke, provide us with the full list of this Messianic line, but the two genealogies listed in Matthew and Luke's Gospels differ from each other on three main points: 1) Matthew begins with Abraham and works *forward* to Jesus, while Luke begins with Jesus and works *backward* to Adam; 2) Luke includes the qualifying parenthetical phrase, "(as was supposed)" when listing Joseph as Jesus' father (though Joseph was *not* Jesus' *natural* father); and 3) beginning with the generation immediately after David, Matthew lists Solomon as the next in line, while Luke lists Nathan as the next in line. Since the primary concern is about determining Jesus' actual lineage, most scholars, including John Wesley, E. W. Bullinger, Charles Ryrie, and Cyrus Schofield, believe Luke's genealogical list is that of Mary, His mother, while Matthew's genealogical list is that of Joseph, the husband of Mary and Jesus' legal male guardian who took the role of His earthly adoptive father.

Because of the Jewish restriction at that time against entering a woman's name in the direct genealogy, these Bible commentators explain that the phrase "Joseph, the son of Heli" in Luke 3:23 more likely refers to Joseph's being the *son-in-law* of Heli (thus taking the place of Mary in the direct genealogical list), since Matthew's genealogy lists *Jacob* as Joseph's father (Matthew 1:16).[14] This further explains the disparity between the lists of names in the two genealogies following King David. Since Joseph was descended from Solomon and Mary was descended from Nathan (both sons of David by his wife Bathsheba; compare with 1 Chronicles 3:1-9), we can see Jesus' qualification both legally (through Joseph) and personally (through Mary) to be the long-awaited Messiah.

Moreover, Luke's genealogical list is especially insightful that Jesus is not only descended from David and Abraham, but His descent from Adam is plainly shown, too. Thus, Jesus' identification as the Second Adam (as the Apostle Paul wrote so eloquently about in 1 Corinthians 15:45-49) is also clearly established here in Luke's genealogy.

The End of the Line

Once Jesus was born to fulfill God's prophecy of a forever King, the Messiah, there was no further need of a genealogical line, so Jesus neither married nor produced any biological children while He was on earth, though we who have experienced the new birth are *all* His spiritual children, as well as His siblings and joint-heirs (compare Hebrews 2:9-13; John 14:8-9; and Romans 8:14-17). Jesus' arrival on the scene is quite literally *the end of the line*—the genealogical line for the Messiah, that is. Since Jesus will never die again, there is no need for a successor, because He is our forever King. As the prophet Isaiah wrote:

> For unto us a Child is born, Unto us a Son is given; **And the government will be upon His shoulder. And His name will be called Wonderful, Counselor, Mighty God, Everlasting Father, Prince of Peace. Of the increase of His government and peace There will be no end, Upon the throne of David and over His kingdom, To order it and establish it with judgment and justice From that time forward, even forever.**

The zeal of the Lord of hosts will perform this. (Isaiah 9:6-7; emphasis added).

The Good News is that not only will Jesus live and reign forever, but we will live and reign *with* Him forever as well! Therefore, we have no further need of children to succeed us either, hence the revelation from Jesus that after our resurrection into the Kingdom, we "neither marry nor are given in marriage" anymore (Matthew 22:30; Mark 12:25; and Luke 20:35) because we have become the Bride of Christ.

Of course, Jesus has not yet taken His seat upon His eternal throne, but that event is not far into the future from now. First, God must subject His enemies under Jesus' feet and put an end to sin once and for all (see Daniel 9:24; Psalm 8:3-6; Psalm 110:1; and 1 Corinthians 15:22-28). That event won't occur until the very end of Jesus' millennial reign (Revelation 20:1-15). I don't know about you, but that day can't come soon enough for me!

Now that we understand how the Messiah came into being, we'll look next at why He is named Jesus Christ. What difference does it make what His name is anyway, just so long as He saves us? Well, let's give that some careful consideration in the next chapter.

CHAPTER FIVE: WHAT'S IN A NAME?

In Shakespeare's classic tragedy, *Romeo and Juliet*, we find the leading lady, Juliet, on her balcony musing about the meaning and application of her new love interest's name: Romeo. The feud between her family, the Capulets, and Romeo's family, the Montagues, is at the root of why she mourns his name and asks ruefully,

> O Romeo, Romeo! wherefore art thou Romeo?
> Deny thy father and refuse thy name. . . .
> 'Tis but thy name that is my enemy. . . .
> What's a Montague? . . . O, be some other name!
> What's in a name? that which we call a rose
> By any other name would smell as sweet. . . .[15]

Of all the Shakespearean lines, perhaps the first line and the final two lines in the above quote are the most familiar to us. They are among the most-quoted lines in literature. Moreover, the question at the beginning of the final two lines quoted above is what I have selected for the title and focus of this chapter's topic: What's in a name?

That's a good question and one which certainly deserves some careful consideration. While Juliet (or maybe it was Shakespeare using Juliet's persona) appears to be suggesting that names are basically superficial and thereby unimportant, God's Word certainly differs with that assessment. All throughout the holy Scriptures, names—especially regarding their meaning—have major significance. Thus, with that in mind, I want to consider a few of the names of God in this chapter and why they are so significant, but first, let's consider the importance of having a name before we proceed.

What Is Your Name?

Usually, the very first question we ask one another when meeting for the first time is, "What is your name?" We want to know this bit of information for multiple reasons. Most importantly, we want to know how to address this new acquaintance, but we also want to get a hint at his or her origin and place in the world. Therefore, while a name may offer us a handle of address, it also often prompts us to prejudge another based on preconceived notions about one's family, national origin, reputation, etc. We may even feel tempted to poke fun at someone with a name that sounds humorous or unusual. Sometimes, we will attach another name (a nickname) to one whom we wish either to endear or disdain. Moreover, someone who develops a bad reputation because of an unkind, or even criminal, act brings disrepute upon his name, and everyone else who possesses that same name is said to have been given "a bad name."

There's much more to a name than its mere spelling and pronunciation. Indeed, every name is rooted in another word or phrase or even a sentence that is fraught with meaning (unless it is a completely fabricated and contrived name, as some mothers are wont to do nowadays).

Although it is likely that many parents name their children with little or no knowledge or understanding of the meaning of their names, their names have meaning, nonetheless. For instance, the ever-popular name of Mary is rooted in the Hebrew word *marah*, which means *bitter* (see Exodus 15:23 and Ruth 1:20). I imagine most parents name their daughters Mary because of Jesus' mother being named Mary, but few stop to consider its real meaning and whether they really want their daughters to be named "Bitter." Most likely, Jesus' mother was named Miryam (see Luke 1:30 CJB), as was a lot of other women during that time, because of the national bitterness they were experiencing under Roman rule. Consider, too, the importance of what God was saying by having His Son, Jesus, born of a woman named *Bitter*. In other words, God's Son was born out of bitterness!

If you don't know the meaning of your own name, I strongly recommend you research it to learn about it, since it has more bearing on your life than you might think. Two excellent Websites to discover the meanings of names are Behind the Name (http://www.behindthename.com/) and Meaning of Names (http://www.meaning-of-names.com/). You may even want to consider legally changing your name if your present name is more of a curse than a blessing!

There are several examples of name changes in the Bible, beginning with Abram (which means *exalted father*), whom God renamed Abraham (which means *father of many*) once it was time for Abraham to move into the promise God had made to him some 24 years earlier (see Genesis 17:5). Because God named Isaac before he was born, there was no need to change his name later to fulfill his destiny, since he was already living out his destiny according to God's plan. However, when it was time for Jacob to return to the Promised Land and resume residence there as a rightful patriarch, God changed his name to Israel (Genesis 32:28 & 35:10), and that is the name by which his descendants are known to this day: the children of Israel.

In Bible times, parents often named their children for something they did at birth (such as Jacob did by grabbing his brother Esau's heel during birth–the name Jacob means something like "heel grabber") or because of their physical appearance (such as Esau, which literally means "hairy," because he was very hairy on his body). Furthermore, Esau was also nicknamed Edom, which means "red," because the stew for which he sold his birthright was red (Genesis 25:29-30). I am uncertain who gave him that nickname, but I doubt he would have liked it, since it would have been a continual reminder of how he lost his birthright.

Others, like Jabez (which means "pain"), were stigmatized by a name that represented the pain they had caused their mothers during childbirth or some other disappointment (see 1 Chronicles 4:9-10). Perhaps this explains why the Scripture tells us God will give us a new name when we enter His eternal Kingdom (see Revelation 2:17; 3:12; and Isaiah 62:2). It will be a good and glorious name chosen by God Himself, and it will last forever! As wise King Solomon wrote, "A *good* name is to be chosen rather than great riches, Loving favor rather than silver and gold" (Proverbs 22:1).

What Is God's Name?

Since names are so important to God, we might ask the question, "What is God's name?" Moses asked God for His name when speaking with Him at the burning bush on Mt. Sinai, although he couched it in such a way as to make it appear the people of Israel would be wanting to know it (Exodus 3:13-15). For all we know, they *might* have asked this question, but interestingly enough, Moses does not record anyone besides himself *ever* asking this question *anywhere* throughout the entire Torah (also called the Pentateuch–the first five books of the Bible), all which Moses wrote.

Strangely, though, Moses first uses the personal name for God (as revealed in Exodus 3:15) in telling the story of creation in Genesis 2:4, and he continues to use it throughout the book of Genesis, yet it was evidently not revealed in the chronological narrative of the Bible until Moses' unexpected meeting with God at the burning bush on Mt. Sinai. Furthermore, although it appears from the text that Abraham called upon God using His personal name when he built an altar and offered a sacrifice to God (Genesis 12:8), it is not until Exodus 6:3 that we learn from God Himself that He was not known by His personal name to any people before Moses, *including* Abraham, Isaac, and Jacob.

Since God's personal name is usually disguised and thereby concealed from us in the English translation of the Bible, before we can fully understand when we're reading the actual personal name of God in the English translation, we must first understand that the translators have substituted the actual name of God with the word "LORD."[16] They spell it in all caps to distinguish it from the actual word "lord" that is sometimes used for God and sometimes used for men. Why do they do this?

According to Dr. William Smith, this practice "was founded upon an erroneous rendering of Leviticus 24:16 from which it was inferred that the mere utterance of the name constituted a capital offence."[17] Yet we must ask, "Why did God give us His name, and even tell us to use His name when swearing an oath? Why does He instruct us to *call* upon His name if He never intended for us to speak or pronounce it?" (See Deuteronomy 6:13; 10:20; and 1 Chronicles 16:8.) Moreover, I think the English translators have done us a great disservice by doing this, since they have *removed* the personal name of God from the holy Scriptures! I hope that does not qualify for the judgment given in Revelation 22:18-19!

So, when Moses asked for God's name at the burning bush, God told him, ". . .'I AM WHO I AM.' And He said, 'Thus you shall say to the children of Israel, 'I AM has sent me to you'" (Exodus 3:14). The actual Hebrew wording here (transliterated) is: "HaYah asher haYah." According to *Strong's Exhaustive Concordance*, the Hebrew words *HaYah* (pronounced ha-YAH) literally mean *the I AM,* and the word *asher* (pronounced ash-ER) may be translated either as *who, which, what,* or *that* in English.[18] I think the original King James may have translated this more clearly as *that,* however, since I think by saying, "I AM THAT I AM," God meant He is a particular entity named I AM. Therefore, He is *that* I AM. Indeed, I don't think it would be incorrect to say it could also mean, "I AM *THE* I AM."

Thus, God's personal name is I AM, although it is expanded from YAH to YAHVEY (or YAHWEH), which means *I AM the Self-Existent One.* While scholars have translated it as JEHOVAH, a better transliteration is YAHOVAH or YAHAVAH, which means *I AM the Breathing, Living One.* Because the correct sound of the initial letter in this name is like the English "Y" sound, and because there is no "J" letter or sound in Hebrew (or in Greek or Latin, for that matter), we should therefore translate this letter as "Y" in English.

Understanding God's name to mean I AM makes so much more sense when we see God's name compounded with other terms, such as Provider, Banner, Peace, etc., because we can get a meaningful statement from it. For instance, Abraham assigns the name of Provider to God (*Yahovah Yireh*, which literally means "I AM seeing to it") after God provided the ram caught in the thicket for the sacrifice in place of Isaac on Mt. Moriah (Genesis 22:14). Therefore, we could translate God's compound name here as *I AM your Provider*, or *I AM Provision*. In fact, the same is true with *all* of God's compound names: Yahovah Nissi (*I AM your Banner*; Exodus 17:15); Yahovah Shalom (*I AM your Peace*; Judges 6:24); and so forth.[19]

Using this understanding, we can now see how the name Yahveh Elohim (pronounced YAH-vay El-oh-HEEM and translated as "LORD God" throughout the Old Testament) may be literally translated as *I AM God* or even, *I AM the Living God*. Furthermore, just as they shortened Elohim to El, they also shortened the name Yahveh to Yah. Consider the passage in Isaiah below for an example where both instances appear.

> Behold,[H2009] God[H410] *is* my salvation;[H3444] I will trust,[H982] and not[H3808] be afraid:[H6342] for[H3588] the LORD[H3050] JE-HOVAH[H3068] *is* my strength[H5797] and *my* song;[H2176] he also is become[H1961] my salvation[H3444] (Isaiah 12:2 KJV+).[20]

The superscripted numbers here are from *Strong's Exhaustive Concordance* for the Hebrew text; hence, they begin with the letter "H." Where you see the first instance of the word "God[H410]" the original Hebrew text uses the word "El," and where you see the word "LORD[H3050]" the original Hebrew text uses "Yah." Therefore, we might read the text in English this way:

"See, God is my salvation; I will trust and not be afraid: for I AM—I AM the Living One—is my strength and my song; He also is become my salvation."

Incidentally, the Hebrew word translated as *salvation* both times in this verse is *yeshua* (pronounced yeh-SHOO-ah; Strong's H3444; יְשׁוּעָה).[21] This is one of the Hebrew variants for the name of Joshua (translated as Jesus from the Greek).

When people of the Bible honored God by naming their children using God's name, they would use the shortened versions for Elohim and Yahvey (El and Yah, respectively). For instance, the name "Michael" (which means, *"Who is like God?"*) ends with "El," the word for "God." However, the name "Michaiah" (also spelled "Micaiah" in 1 Kings 22:8, which means, *"Who is like Yahvey?"*) is the same name, except with the ending of "Yah," the personal name of God. Thus, Hebrew names which end with "El" (such as Daniel, Ezekiel, Joel, etc.) include the name of God in their meaning, while names which end with "Yah" (such as Isaiah, Hananiah, Zechariah, etc.) include the name of Yahvey in their meaning. Of course, the same may be done by placing El or Yah at the beginning of a name, such as Eli, Elisha, or Joshua (pronounced either Yah-SHOO-ah or Yah-ho-SHOO-ah; see Strong's H3091; יְהוֹשׁוּעַ).[22]

So, What's in a Name?

Names have definite meaning, and that meaning is evidently meaningful to God, if to no one else. According to an instructional

DVD by evangelist Perry Stone, if we pay careful attention, God sends us messages hidden within the meaning of various names. For instance, for the first ten generations in Genesis from Adam to Noah, we learn that we can compose a sentence with a message in it using the names given there. In chronological order, these names are Adam, Seth, Enos, Cainan, Mahalaleel, Jared, Enoch, Methuselah, Lamech, and Noah. I have listed their various meanings below:

Adam = Man
Seth = Appointed or Substitute
Enos = Mortal or Dedicated
Cainan = Sorrow, Acquired or Possession
Mahalaleel = The Blessed God or The Praise of God
Jared = Descend, Descent or Come Down
Enoch = Teacher or Teaching
Methuselah = His Death Will Bring
Lamech = Despairing or Lowly
Noah = Rest

When you put these meanings together, you can form a sentence: "Man is appointed mortal sorrow, [sic] the Blessed God will descend teaching; his death will bring the despairing rest."[23] Creation science proponent Paul Taylor writes it this way in his book *The Six Days of Genesis*: "Man is appointed mortal sorrow, but the God who is to be praised shall come down, teaching that his death shall bring the despairing rest."[24] Yet another possibility, which I put forth on my own, might be: "Mankind's Substitute is dedicated and acquired through praise of God and will descend teaching that His death will bring the lowly rest." It does not require enormous intelligence to perceive that this is the Gospel Story encapsulated in one sentence and hidden at the very beginning of both the Bible and human history.

While this is quite intriguing, it is only the beginning (pardon the pun). All throughout the Scriptures, names carry great meaning, just waiting for discovery by the astute researcher. When we get to the New Testament Scriptures, however, we run into the obstacle of multi-lingual translation, meaning we are reading the translation of a translation (i.e., from Hebrew to Greek to English), because the New Testament was written by Jewish men who spoke Aramaic and Hebrew and wrote their testimonies in Koine Greek, which was later translated into contemporary English (among many other languages). Thus, all the familiar Hebrew names of the Old Testament are disguised to some degree when written in the Greek New Testament and translated into English from Greek, instead of being translated into English from Hebrew. Several are altered significantly enough to make them unrecognizable to us. For instance, Jacob becomes James (though it should be translated as Jacobus, since that was the actual Hellenized name), Johanan (or Jochanan) becomes John, Eleazar becomes Lazarus, and Joshua becomes Jesus. Keep in mind, too, that all these Hebrew names containing a "J" initial in English should actually be spelled with a "Y" for the initial. While some names are still somewhat recognizable (such as Judas for Judah, Simon for Simeon, Elias for Elijah, and Esaias for Isaiah), it still requires a bit of deduction to decipher. Nevertheless, we need to reverse the translation process from Greek to Hebrew, and then into English, before we can understand the true Hebrew meaning of the names.

To demonstrate two examples of what happens when we don't have the original, more familiar Hebrew name to go by, read Acts 7:45 and Hebrews 4:8 in the King James Version of the Bible. In both these cases, the name Jesus refers to Joshua, the man who succeeded Moses as leader of Israel. Though it is rightly translated from the Greek to English as Jesus in both cases, it causes confusion for the contemporary English reader, since Jesus is the name we have come to associate with the Son of God, our Lord and Savior alone. What we fail to understand, however, is that Jesus' Hebrew name was Joshua (literally, Yahshua, though most spell the translation as Yeshua), and He wasn't the first to be given this name. Besides Joshua the son of Nun, who was the successor to Moses and the first person with this name mentioned in the Scriptures, we find at least three other men named Joshua in the Old Testament. There was Joshua the Bethshemite in whose field the Ark of the Covenant was returned by the Philistines (1 Samuel 6:18); there was Joshua the governor of the city under King Josiah's rule (perhaps we would call him the mayor of Jerusalem today; 2 Kings 23:8); and there was Joshua the son of Josedech, who was the High Priest immediately following the return from the Babylonian Exile (Haggai 1:1; 2:1-2; and Zechariah 3:1).

So, this brings us to the question of what are the meanings of the names of Joshua and Jesus? Since Joshua appears to contain the personal name of God (Yah) compounded with the Hebrew word for salvation (yeshua), it literally means *I AM Salvation*. In fact, of the five Hebrew words used in the Old Testament for the English word *salvation* in the KJV, the most frequently used word by far is *yeshua* (65 times out of 119 by my count).[25] Thus, if anyone should ever challenge you to point out Jesus' name in the Old Testament, besides pointing them to the four men who are named Joshua (not to mention the variations on that name: Hoshea, Oshea, Hosea, Jehoshua, Jeshua, and Isaiah), you can also point them to the very word for salvation in the Hebrew text: *yeshua*, which is the very name Jeshua, also written as Joshua, and better known to us today as Jesus.

So, what does the name of Jesus really mean? According to *Vine's Complete Expository Dictionary of Old and New Testament Words*, "iesous (G2424) is a transliteration of the Heb. 'Joshua,' meaning 'Jehovah is salvation'. . . ."[26] Therefore, Jesus means *Salvation*, or more accurately in Hebrew, it means *I AM Salvation*. This explains why the angel, speaking to Joseph in a dream, told him,

> . . ."Joseph, son of David, do not be afraid to take to you Mary your wife, for that which is conceived in her is of the Holy Spirit. And she will bring forth a Son, and **you shall call His name JESUS, for He will save His people from their sins**" (Matthew 1:20-21; emphasis added).

For the average believer, this statement in Matthew's Gospel has effectively "gone over" our collective heads and left us suspecting that it is because Jesus was sent to be "the Savior of the world" that He is given this name, but coming to that conclusion overlooks the true meaning of Jesus' name and leaves us with a misunderstanding of it. While it is true that Jesus is a Savior, it is important for us to know that He is a Savior *because* He is the very *epitome* of salvation. Therefore, He is *more* than a Savior; He *is* Salvation. As the Apostle Peter said, "Nor is there salvation in any other, for there is no other name under heaven given among men by which we must be saved" (Acts 4:12).

Salvation By A Name?

For several years now, phrases like "believed in the name" (John 3:18), "no other name . . . by which we must be saved" (Acts 4:12), "whoever calls on the name . . . shall be saved" (Acts 2:21; Romans 10:13), etc. have seemed to leap off the page and demand an explanation in my mind. What does it mean to *believe in* or to *call upon the name of* Jesus? Well, now that we understand what the name of Jesus truly means, it all comes clear. We are saved by believing (i.e., trusting) in the name that means *Salvation*. In other words, we expect that the One who epitomizes salvation in both name and deeds will save us according to His promise. Once we establish a relationship with Him—simply by humbly and sincerely asking for it—we are then assured of receiving whatever we ask of Him by abiding (i.e., continuing) in Him ever after (John 15:7).

For now, suffice it to say that by calling upon the name that means salvation to save us from whatever trouble in which we may find ourselves (e.g., sin, sickness, dangerous evildoers, demonic attacks, etc.), we can expect deliverance. There's great power in this name because of what the One who bears this name has accomplished *for* us and promised *to* us (see Matthew 28:18).

What About Jesus' *Other* Name?

Is the name of Jesus the only name we ought to consider here? What about Jesus' *other* name? When we think of the name of Jesus, we usually include His divine title—Christ—as a surname. So, what about *this* name? What does *Christ* mean?

The name Christ comes from the Greek word Christos (pronounced kris-TAHS; Strong's G5547; Χριστός),[27] and it means "anointed" or "anointed one." However, this word equates to the Hebrew word *Mashiach* (pronounced mah-SHEE-akh; Strong's H4899; מָשִׁיחַ),[28] which also means "anointed" or "anointed one."

Though I do not profess to be a Greek or Hebrew scholar by *any* stretch of the imagination, one fact that seems to have been overlooked in this word is that when translated into English as Messiah, it appears to contain the personal name of God (Yah) at the end. Is this merely a translational mistake or is it an oversight of historic proportions?

Since the root word for *mashiach* is *mashach* (pronounced mah-SHAHK; Strong's H4886; מָשַׁח),[29] which also means *anointed*, adding the "Yah" sound to the word appears to be adding God's personal name to it. Therefore, I think it should literally read *I AM Anointed,* or *I AM the Anointed One.* This makes much more sense when we reverse the name to Christ Jesus, as the Apostle Paul does throughout his epistles. When we do this, the meaning now reads: *I AM Anointed Salvation,* or even *I AM Anointed for Salvation.* I am inclined to think that the Apostle Paul wrote it this way with this meaning in mind. In fact, except for only two instances in one of the Apostle Peter's epistles (in 1 Peter 5:10 & 14), Paul appears to be the only one who used Jesus' name in this way. That fact alone makes it worth noting and studying further.

Understanding the meaning of names and other key words in Scripture can add a great deal to our insight and knowledge of God's Word. Having such insight can make all the difference in having an accurate comprehension of God's intentions for including certain facts and ideas in His Word. Such is true regarding the topic we will discuss in the next chapter. Just what does predestination mean and how are we to apply it to our knowledge of God and the salvation which He has made available to us? Keep reading to find out.

CHAPTER SIX: THE QUESTION OF PREDESTINATION

One of the most debated doctrines in all the Bible is the doctrine of predestination. Why is this? It is because it affects not only our understanding of salvation and how we believe we are saved, but it affects the security of our salvation, too. In this chapter, I hope to alleviate some (if not all) of this misunderstanding for those who are truly seeking the truth about this matter by using the plain Word of God. However, if you already have your mind made up and have no intention of considering any other possibility besides your own present interpretation, then you might as well skip this chapter and move on to the next, since my explanation will not likely change your mind.

Is Predestination Actually in the Bible?

Many freewill-believing Christians doubt that the concept of predestination is even in the Bible. After all, wouldn't such a fact negate the free will choice of anyone to believe? Well, if correctly understood, no, it wouldn't.

I, too, believe in the free will of every believer to choose salvation for himself or herself based on clear Scriptural evidence, but the Scriptural evidence for the doctrine of predestination cannot be denied or ignored either. Therefore, how we understand this fact about God and His Plan of Salvation as it relates to predestination makes all the difference. Misunderstanding this concept will likely cause us great fear and consternation at the least and a precarious endangerment of our soul at the worst, so let's see if we can clarify this a bit more.

Although the word *predestination* does not appear in any of the 15 English translations of the Bible that I checked, the word *predestined* appears four separate times in the New King James Version (the primary version I have used throughout this book)—twice in Paul's letter to the Romans and twice in his letter to the Ephesians. Instead of using the word *predestined*, however, *The American Standard Version* uses the word "foreordained" and *Young's Literal Translation* uses the word "fore-appoint." While a few others use various other phrases, such as "marked out" (*The Bible in Basic English*), "already decided to choose" (*Contemporary English Version*), "determined in advance" (*Complete Jewish Bible*), and "set apart" (*The Good News Bible*), the rest I checked use either "predestinate," "predestinated" or "predestined."[30] The Greek word from which all of these words and phrases are translated is *proorizo* (pronounced pro-or-ID-zoh; Strong's G4309; προορίζω),[31] which means "to limit in advance" or "predetermine." Now that we know the doctrine of predestination is indeed in the Bible, how do we apply this knowledge to the salvation of our soul?

Keeping It in Context

Before we can properly understand and apply the doctrine of predestination to salvation, we must first put it in context with the rest of God's character, since a misapplication of this idea could easily result in a mischaracterization of God. Thus, we need to examine this doctrine in view of God's good character to correctly understand and apply it and thereby avoid a terrible misrepresentation of God.

As we learned from Chapter 1, God is righteous (meaning just or fair, as well as without wrongdoing), omniscient (meaning all-knowing), generous, merciful, and gracious, among many other things. Therefore, in whatever way we define and explain predestination as a work of God, we must do so with God's unchanging and unchangeable character in mind. In other words, since God is righteous (or just and fair), we know that He would not treat anyone in an unjust (or unrighteous and unfair) manner. He would not only set up fair rules for us to follow, but He would follow His own rules of fairness. Thus, He demonstrates that He has great integrity. Moreover, because He is also omniscient, He already knows ahead of time how everything is going to turn out, so He can make His plans and take His actions accordingly. Also, because He is generous, He is not sparing with anything He gives or does, including the provision of good things and ample opportunities for us to choose good things, such as mercy, grace, life, health, peace, and joy. Finally, because God is merciful (i.e., withholding or lessening punishment when we act ignorantly or when we confess and repent of wrongdoing) and gracious (i.e., giving us blessings we don't deserve, didn't earn, and can't afford), this must mean that He not only *wants* what's best for us, but He also *does* what's best for us without our even being aware of it, let alone asking for it.

Placing predestination within this context of God's revealed and unchanging character helps us see first that God simply *could not* arbitrarily choose some of us to save and others of us to condemn without any input from either, as some have purported, because this would make God unjust. How is it fair to predestine one for salvation and another for condemnation when neither is given the opportunity to decide for himself or herself what he or she really wants? Why give human beings the power to choose some things but deny them the power to choose the most significant thing: eternal life with Him? What if the one chosen for condemnation would rather be saved, and what if the one saved would rather have been rejected than spend eternity with a God he or she personally rejects? Moreover, why would God want to choose someone to spend eternity with Him who hates Him, and why would He reject someone for eternity who loves Him? Not only is this unjust, but it simply makes no sense!

Indeed, all those who reject God, and are then rejected *by* God, will realize their foolish blunder once they are cast into the Lake of Fire, but the time and opportunity for believing God's Word and choosing life with God will have permanently passed by that time. It's no wonder that Jesus says, "There shall be weeping, wailing, and gnashing of teeth" (Matthew 8:12; 13:42 & 50; 22:13; 24:51; 25:30; and Luke 13:28).

When we consider God's omniscience, however, we can much more easily understand how God is able to predestine people for eternal life with Him or eternal damnation in Hell. How? Because God knows in advance (foreknows) who will believe and accept His Word and who will disbelieve and reject His Word. It really is just that simple. Therefore, God can rightly predestine someone for eternity based on the decision God knows far in advance that this person will make, because God knows what each person's *final decision* will be. Predestining someone in this manner is not fate, since it is not God who decides *for* an individual, but rather it is God's sovereign act based on *the individual's decision* that God has permitted him or her to make and which He is able to foreknow in His omniscience. To claim something else is to misinterpret and misapply the truth of God's Word, to unnecessarily overcomplicate an otherwise straightforward doctrine, and to completely misrepresent God's unchangeably fair and just nature as being *unfair* and *unrighteous*.

Faith or Fatalism?

So, how does the doctrine of predestination avoid being labeled fatalistic, and how does faith fit in with the doctrine of predestination? It's simple. As I've already explained above, since God does not make a person's decision *for* him or her without any input *from* him or her, it cannot be defined as fate.

Webster's online dictionary defines "fate" in several ways, but the two which convey the most widely-used meaning are as follows: "a power that is believed to control what happens in the future . . . 2 a: an inevitable and often adverse outcome, condition, or end."[32] Therefore, because every human being has a free will to choose whatever he or she wants, everyone can choose whether to place faith in God and His revealed and written Word—the Bible—or whether to dismiss both as unbelievable and reject them.

Everything we need to know about God, ourselves, and the world He has created for us may be found in the Bible. Furthermore, there are many facts and truths that are hidden in the Bible for us to enjoy searching out. It's a little like a scavenger hunt where we find clues about a treasure in one place which leads us to discover truth about the treasure in another place. God has even included this fact in the pages of the Bible for us. For instance, "It is the glory of God to conceal a matter, But the glory of kings is to search out a matter" (Proverbs 25:2). Does the fact that I am not presently a king sitting on a throne thereby disqualify me from either searching or being able to discover the concealed facts and truths in the Bible? No, because we ascertain from two other Scripture verses that God has made *all* His people (i.e., those who have chosen and accepted an eternal relationship with Him) to be both kings and priests unto Him (Revelation 1:6 &

5:10). These are just a few verses hidden in plain sight amidst the more than 31,000 total verses in the canonized English Bible (depending on the version of the Bible you use for your count).[33]

Since God has predestined us for eternal life with Him, because He already knows we will choose Him for our God and Savior, what role do we and our faith play in this plan? If it's a foregone conclusion that we will be saved by God's sovereign predestination, why do we need to do anything at all? You see, that's the crux of the misunderstanding about the doctrine of predestination. As I just stated above, it is *not a fatalistic* predestination, but a predestination based on a *foreknown decision* derived from divine omniscience. If we don't take the step of faith and believe God's Word and accept God's offer of redemption and salvation, then we will have failed to actively choose Him and His Plan of Salvation for us. We will therefore be rejected and lost because we have effectively rejected God and His Plan of Salvation. We must therefore personally and *deliberately choose* to believe in and accept the Plan of Salvation made possible for us by God through His only begotten Son, Jesus Christ, *so that* we may be predestined for eternal life with Him. Without making this decision we will *not* be predestined for eternal life with Him, but rather, we will be predestined for the eternal damnation of Hell *without* Him. We *absolutely must choose* to believe in and accept God's only option for salvation or we will be condemned, lost, and separated from Him forever (John 3:18 and John 14:6).

How do we know this, and how do we know *what* to believe in to be saved? What is the truth? It's very simple. We can answer each of these questions with the same response: *The Holy Bible*. Since *The Holy Bible* contains God's Word, we can believe what it says and accept it as truth.

What Is Truth?

Pilate asked Jesus this question when Jesus stood before him for judgment. He obviously thought it was a rhetorical question, because he didn't wait for Jesus to answer before he turned and walked away. Little did Pilate know that the Truth was standing right in front of him (John 1:1, 14, 17; 14:6; & 17:17)! As we read in John 17 the words of Jesus' prayer to God for His disciples the night before, He provides us with the answer to this question: "Sanctify them by Your truth. **Your word is truth**" (John 17:17; emphasis added).

If we want to know the truth about *anything*, we must seek it in God's Word, because that is where the truth resides. Jesus said so. Moreover, according to the Apostle John, Jesus *is* God's Word in human flesh (John 1:1 & 14). Therefore, anything which contradicts God's Word *cannot* be the truth. This has been Satan's unchanging strategy since the temptation of Eve in the garden. He begins by casting doubt on what God has said by asking, "Has God indeed said . . .?" (Genesis 3:1). Then when he finds us misquoting or misapplying God's Word, as Eve did (compare Genesis 2:16-17 with Genesis 3:3), he proceeds by contradicting God's

Word (Genesis 3:4). So, to avoid being deceived about the truth, we need to *know* the truth. How can we know the truth? Again, we learn the truth from reading and meditating on God's Word. There is God's Word, and then there is any other word which differs from or contradicts God's Word. It's our choice which to believe, and it's just that simple!

The first step to learning and knowing the truth, then, is getting as much of God's Word into us as we can. Those who either do not know God's Word, or who do not know it well, are easy targets of Satan's perversions of God's truth. It's very easy to trick someone who has rarely, if ever, read the Bible simply by giving them an erroneous quotation from the Bible, such as "God helps those who help themselves." It's stunning how many people actually believe this statement is in the Bible! Once you have carefully read through the entire Bible at least one time, however, you will be more aware of what's really in it. Of course, the more times you read it, the more familiar you will become with its contents and the harder it will be for anyone to trick or deceive you with a false claim.

The same is true with discerning the truth about other claims, such as supposedly scientific evidence for one thing or another which conflicts with or contradicts the Bible. For instance, the theory of evolution and the calculation of the age of the universe based on presumptive trends like carbon dating can be easily refuted by the simple presentation of the truth of God's Word. The Genesis account of creation in six days handily refutes the theory of evolution, and the calculation of time since the creation event easily refutes the "old earth" theory. Since God has told us this is how everything happened, imposing anything more onto the text which is not plainly revealed to us in the Genesis account makes God into a liar. Since none of us were there, including Moses who transcribed God's account, we must simply take God's Word for it. If a gap of billions of years had occurred between Genesis 1:1 and Genesis 1:2, then God would have plainly told us so.

Rightly interpreting the truth about the doctrine of predestination is just as dependent on God's Word. Since God has clearly told us through the Apostle Paul that He predestined those He foreknew (Romans 8:29), and because God has described His character throughout the Bible as being omniscient, righteous, and full of mercy, love, and grace, then we can conclude that the only right way to understand the doctrine of predestination is by describing it as a sovereign act of God based on His omniscience. For God to force His will on us after granting us a free will of our own (which He gave us for the express purpose of choosing or rejecting eternal life with Him) is simply preposterous! Such a conclusion turns God into a monstrous Being whose Word we just can't trust. How utterly futile (from our perspective, at least) for Him to command us to choose Him when He has already decided to reject us anyway! Consider how unfair and unrighteous it would be for God to tell us to choose whether we will serve Him (see Joshua 24:15) when He has already chosen to condemn us, whether we choose Him or not. On the flip side, how unfair and unrighteous would it be for God to tell us to choose whether we will serve Him only to save us anyway, even after we've rejected Him? Not only would this be unfair, but it would be very unloving for Him to reject us after we've chosen and accepted Him.

My friend and fellow author Gil VanOrder, Jr. has written a magnificent refutation of this sort of theology in his book *Considering Calvinism: Faith or Fatalism?* I highly recommend this work to you regardless of your position on predestination heretofore. It will truly open your eyes to more than just the doctrine of predestination. It will also give you an entirely different perspective on the writings of Protestant Reformers John Calvin and Martin Luther, not to mention those of more contemporary authors like R. C. Sproul and John MacArthur. Reading their perspectives in their own words and according to their personal actions (in the case of Calvin and Luther) leaves little doubt about their true thoughts and convictions.

Perhaps the major reason the doctrine of predestination is so misunderstood in the Church today is because of the misinterpretation and misapplication by theologians like Calvin who completely skew the whole thing. Moreover, the primary reason it is such a rejected and maligned doctrine by believers in free will is because of this erroneous teaching by Calvin and others. There can be no denying that predestination is a fact in the Scriptures, but properly interpreting and applying it makes all the difference in our proper understanding of it and our proper understanding of how we are saved by God.

While the doctrine of predestination can be confusing to Christians, the teaching of the unpardonable sin is almost equally as confusing *and* frightening. Indeed, it *should* be frightening, because of its importance to God and the cold finality with which Jesus warns us about it. If you're fearful that you may have committed this unpardonable sin, keep reading to learn more and to settle it in your mind once and forever. We'll consider that teaching in the next chapter.

CHAPTER SEVEN: THE UNPARDONABLE SIN

I've included a discussion of the unpardonable sin in this book because it directly concerns the salvation of our soul every bit as much as the doctrine of predestination and the problem of sin. After all, if God requires us to be cleansed of *all* our sin before we will be permitted into His Kingdom, retaining just *one* unpardoned sin would thereby disqualify us from gaining entrance into His Kingdom. Furthermore, just as predestination is one of the most debated doctrines in the Bible because of misunderstanding its meaning, the unpardonable sin is one of the most feared teachings in the Bible for the same reason. Just as with the doctrine of predestination, we can't deny the existence of the unpardonable sin, because Jesus Himself utters the words which reveal it as a fact.

Many a Christian has been filled with the fear that perhaps he or she has committed this terrible sin and have consequently lived their lives through alternating bouts of dread and reassurance. I will confess to being one of them until I began diligently researching this matter for a more thorough and

clearer understanding. After all, the Apostle Paul recommend-
ed that every believer should work out his or her "own salvation with fear and trembling" (Philippians 2:12). I think he
meant that we should strive to resolve the security of our soul
with the clear understanding that it truly is a life-or-death matter that requires our full, undivided attention and absolute certainty. Therefore, just as we would experience trepidation with
attempting to accomplish a feat upon which something of im-
mense value was depending on our success, we should give
even more diligence to working out our salvation. In the end,
what is more valuable than our soul? Jesus asked this same
question of us (see Mark 8:36-37). Now that I believe I have
attained a more thorough and clearer understanding of this
subject of the unpardonable sin, it is my distinct pleasure to reveal the results of my research and study to you.

What *Is* the Unpardonable Sin?

Before we launch into our discussion, we should first answer
the question of exactly what the unpardonable sin is, so that we
know precisely what we are talking about. Succinctly put, it is
blaspheming the Holy Spirit of God. Jesus introduces this information to us at the point when the religious leaders falsely accused Him of collaborating with Beelzebub (another title for
Satan) to cast out demons. I encourage you to read the entire pe-
ricope of Matthew 12:22-45 to get the full context, but I will quote

only the portion which deals specifically with the unpardonable sin here:

> If Satan casts out Satan, he is divided against himself. How then will his kingdom stand? And if I cast out demons by Beelzebub, by whom do your sons cast them out? Therefore they shall be your judges. But if I cast out demons by the Spirit of God, surely the kingdom of God has come upon you. Or how can one enter a strong man's house and plunder his goods, unless he first binds the strong man? And then he will plunder his house. He who is not with Me is against Me, and he who does not gather with Me scatters abroad. **Therefore I say to you, every sin and blasphemy will be forgiven men, but the blasphemy against the Spirit will not be forgiven men.** Anyone who speaks a word against the Son of Man, it will be forgiven him; **but whoever speaks against the Holy Spirit, it will not be forgiven him, either in this age or in the age to come** (Matthew 12:26-32; emphasis added).

It is that final statement of "it will not be forgiven him, either in this age or in the age to come" that has earned this teaching the title of "the unpardonable sin" and left so many in great fear that they may have unwittingly committed this sin and lost their soul forever. Although Jesus did not give it this title, theologians studying and writing about it ever since have used it. Nevertheless, it appears to be an accurate description of the sin based on Jesus' words in Matthew 12:32. We need to know and understand this fully, however, so that we will be "rightly dividing the word of truth" (2 Timothy 2:15).

To fully understand the nature of this sin, we must first define what the words "blasphemy" and "unpardonable" mean. According to Webster's online dictionary, the word "blasphemy" means "the act of insulting or showing contempt or lack of reverence for God."[34] The word "unpardonable" (because it contains the prefix "un") means "opposite of : contrary to"[35] the word "pardonable"; and the word "pardonable" means "able to be forgiven."[36] Therefore, "unpardonable" means "something which is unable to be forgiven." By this definition, then, blasphemy against the Holy Spirit of God is something which is unable to be forgiven.

But What About the Grace of God?

Anytime someone asserts the biblical truth of an unpardonable sin, it almost always provokes someone else to ask, "But what about the grace of God?" This is a very good question, but there's no getting around the fact that the unpardonable sin exists, since Jesus Himself has stated it so clearly. Personally, I believe that God has instituted this actuality to demonstrate that His grace does, in fact, have a limit and that it is not to be abused or cheapened with a flagrantly sinful lifestyle as the Gnostics and other heretics of history have taught and practiced. Because of God's love, mercy, and grace toward us and His seemingly unlimited ability and willingness to forgive us for any and every sin just for asking, many Christians have developed the attitude that they can do whatever and live any way they choose with no threat to their eternal soul simply because they expect they can always ask for and receive God's forgiveness.

Chapter Seven: The Unpardonable Sin

To illustrate this point briefly, I remember when I was a young, and very new, pastor in my mid-twenties that I went to visit an older adult couple who were newlywed. In fact, I think she was in her late-seventies or early eighties and he was in his mid-eighties. She was from a Pentecostal background, and he was from a Methodist background. She had just learned that she was going to forfeit her deceased first husband's social security benefit now that she had remarried, and because she was unwilling to relinquish it, she had decided to divorce her present husband to get it reinstated. Her concluding statement to me was (to the best of my recollection, at least), "I know I shouldn't get a divorce, but I can just ask God to forgive me, and He will."

Initially, she was seeking my agreement and approval of her reasoning and decision, but when I disagreed and tried to dissuade her, she quickly withdrew from the room and left me to talk with her husband alone. I thought he was remarkably understanding of her feelings, even though her actions clearly demonstrated that she loved that pittance of money more than she loved him, and she was even willing to ignore God's Word as well!

It is this sort of manipulative attitude toward God, either to get what we want, or to justify what we've done in violation of His commandments, or to justify deliberately committing a sin in advance (as this woman did) that belies an obvious ignorance of God's character as described in His Word. Moreover, due to the rampant biblical illiteracy and consequential ignorance of the Scriptures within the Church today, along with the prominent teaching of cheap grace, it may be that most Christians aren't even aware that there *is* such a thing as an unpardonable sin!

Now, although it appears that this woman did not commit the unpardonable sin, she most definitely sinned willfully with the expectation that God would still forgive her. Whether He did, in fact, forgive her is a matter between Him and her and is not something I am qualified to judge. However, according to the letter to the Hebrews we learn,

> **For if we sin willfully after we have received the knowledge of the truth, there no longer remains a sacrifice for sins,** but a certain fearful expectation of judgment, and fiery indignation which will devour the adversaries (Hebrews 10:26-27; emphasis added).

Does this mean we cannot be forgiven for any sin we *willfully* commit after we "receive the knowledge of the truth"? What does it mean to "receive the knowledge of the truth" anyway? It means that once we know without a doubt that Jesus paid for *all* our sins *once and forever*, to continue sinning *willfully* will nullify His atoning sacrifice. Here's how the Book of Hebrews puts it a few verses before and immediately after the verses just quoted above:

> But this Man [Jesus], after He had offered one sacrifice for sins forever, sat down at the right hand of God, from that time waiting till His enemies are made His footstool. For by one offering He has perfected forever those who are being sanctified. . . . **For if we sin willfully after we have received the knowledge of the truth, there no longer remains a sacrifice for sins,** but a certain fearful expectation of judgment,

and fiery indignation which will devour the adversaries. Anyone who has rejected Moses' law dies without mercy on the testimony of two or three witnesses. **Of how much worse punishment, do you suppose, will he be thought worthy who has trampled the Son of God underfoot, counted the blood of the covenant by which he was sanctified a common thing, and insulted the Spirit of grace?** (Hebrews 10:12-14 & 26-29; emphasis added).

This brings us full circle to our original questions now: "What is the unpardonable sin, and how do I know if I have committed this sin?" According to the passage above quoted from Hebrews, when we have "insulted the Spirit of Grace" by disrespecting the Son of God, devaluing His precious blood sacrificed for us, and effectively demeaning the grace of God in the process, it appears we have committed an unpardonable sin. Does this mean then that there is more than one unpardonable sin?

I think what the writer of Hebrews (probably the Apostle Paul) is attempting to clarify for us is that one who claims to be a believer in the One True God and has accepted His Plan of Salvation made available through His Son Jesus Christ yet chooses to continue living a lifestyle of sin in direct and conscious violation of God's Word has made Jesus' blood-atoning sacrifice of no avail to himself or herself. This is an entirely different mindset from someone who is striving to live a life of righteousness according to God's Word yet yields to an occasional sin through the course of daily living. The Apostle Paul explained this dichotomy to us in his letter to the Romans thusly:

For we know that the law [God's commandment] is spiritual, but I am carnal [fleshly], sold under sin. For what I am doing, I do not understand. **For what I will to do, that I do not practice; but what I hate, that I do.** If, then, I do what I will not to do, I agree with the law that it is good. But now, it is no longer I who do it, but sin that dwells in me. For I know that in me (that is, in my flesh) nothing good dwells; for to will is present with me, but how to perform what is good I do not find. **For the good that I will to do, I do not do; but the evil I will not to do, that I practice. Now if I do what I will not to do, it is no longer I who do it, but sin that dwells in me.** I find then a law, that evil is present with me, the one who wills to do good. **For I delight in the law of God according to the inward man. But I see another law in my members, warring against the law of my mind, and bringing me into captivity to the law of sin which is in my members.** O wretched man that I am! Who will deliver me from this body of death? I thank God—through Jesus Christ our Lord! **So then, with the mind I myself serve the law of God, but with the flesh the law of sin** (Romans 7:14-25; emphasis added).

The Apostle Paul was saying that he was struggling against his fleshly desires to do what the law of God commands, yet his flesh would sometimes win this battle and his spirit would sometimes win it. The key point is that he was continuing to *struggle* against his flesh. The *willful* sinner, on the other hand, has given up the struggle altogether and completely given in to the desires of the flesh. A *willful* sinner is one who *deliberately* (that is, *willfully*) breaks God's commandment. As the Apostle James wrote, "Therefore, to him who knows to do good and does not do it, to him it is sin" (James 4:17). While a great many have applied this passage in the Book of James to the "sin of *omission*," it is just as applicable to the "sin of *commission*" in which we willfully violate God's commandment. So, does this mean we can't be forgiven for such willful sins? If that is true, then there is more than one unpardonable sin! In that case, every sin we commit *willfully* becomes an unpardonable sin! No, if a willful sinner who claims to be a Christian chooses to repent of this willful sinfulness, then he or she can once again enjoy the gracious forgiveness of God through the atoning blood of Jesus. The key, of course, is whether this willful sinner can humble himself or herself and truly repent of (turn from) this sin.

A similar example of this behavior and attitude may be found in the Book of Ezekiel where God says:

> "Say to them: 'As I live,' says the Lord GOD, 'I have no pleasure in the death of the wicked, but that the wicked turn from his way and live. Turn, turn from your evil ways! For why should you die, O house of Israel?' Therefore you, O son of man, say to the children of your people: **'The righteousness of the righteous man shall not deliver him in the day of his transgression; as for the wickedness of the wicked, he shall not fall because of it in the day that he turns from his wickedness; nor shall the righteous be able to live because of his righteousness in the day that he sins.'** When I say to the righteous that he shall surely live, but he trusts in his own righteousness and commits iniquity, none of his righteous works shall be remembered; but because of the iniquity that he has committed, he shall die. Again, when I say to the wicked, 'You shall surely die,' if he turns from his sin and does what is lawful and right, if the wicked restores the pledge, gives back what he has stolen, and walks in the statutes of life without committing iniquity, he shall surely live; he shall not die. None of his sins which he has committed shall be remembered against him; he has**

**done what is lawful and right; he shall surely
live"** (Ezekiel 33:11-16; emphasis added).

For those who argue that this passage is Old Testament and
therefore inapplicable to us now, I ask, "Is this the same God
speaking His Word or is it a different God? Where in the New
Testament does Jesus or either of the Scripture writers negate
this methodology, even with the doctrine of salvation by grace
through faith, as depicted in Ephesians 2:8-10? Did God suddenly become a God of grace after Jesus' death and resurrection
or has He *always* been a God of grace? Before the Law of Moses,
did God ever show grace? What about the case of Noah (Genesis
6:5-8)? The Hebrew word *chen* (pronounced CANE, Strong's
H2580, חֵן),[37] which is translated as *grace* in the New King
James Version of this verse, may also be translated as *favor*, but
it means the same either way.

There are several other instances throughout the Old Testament where the grace of God is displayed, including the inter-
view with Cain after God rejected his sacrifice (Genesis 4:6-7)
and again when God marked him to protect him from vengeance
by others (which, ultimately, were his own parents, brothers and
sisters) after he yielded to his flesh and killed his brother, Abel
(Genesis 4:13-16). However, did God suddenly stop showing
grace after He introduced the Law of Moses to the people of Israel? What about the time when King David committed both
adultery and murder? Was David living under the Law of Moses? He most certainly was. Should he have been stoned to death

for his two capital crimes of adultery and murder? The Law of Moses said he should have.

Dating as far back as the time of Noah following the Flood (long before the Law of Moses) God had instituted capital punishment for the crime/sin of murder (Genesis 9:5-6). So, why wasn't David stoned to death for his sins? The only explanation is the grace of God shown to David after he repented. You see, God didn't suddenly become a God of grace in the New Testament. He has *always* been a God of grace.

So, are there now *two* Gods in the Bible: Jesus, the God of the New Testament, and Jehovah (or Yahweh), the God of the Old Testament? If so, are we now permitted to *ignore* the God of the Old Testament? If Jesus is God in human flesh (see John 1:1-3 & 14), is He then the same God as the One in the Old Testament or is He an entirely new and different God in the New Testament? According to Jesus' conversation with Philip on the night before He was crucified, we learn,

> Philip said to Him, "Lord, show us the Father, and it is sufficient for us." Jesus said to him, "Have I been with you so long, and yet you have not known Me, Philip? **He who has seen Me has seen the Father;** so how can you say, 'Show us the Father'?" (John 14:8-9; emphasis added).

If Jesus is therefore the same unchangeable God that has always existed, it's no wonder the Book of Hebrews states emphatically, "Jesus Christ is the same yesterday, today, and forever" (Hebrews 13:8). What does *yesterday* mean in this verse? It represents the past, which reaches back not only to Jesus' birth but into eternity itself.

Jesus is not a distinct and separate God from Yahweh, the Father God. He is Father, Son and Holy Spirit all together–the Triune God. Perhaps now this can put to rest the incredulous query of how God, the Father, could so willingly sacrifice His Son for the sins of humanity. It is because God is sacrificing *Himself* for us! Who else could say the following with any kind of authority?

> **No one takes it [my life] from Me, but I lay it down of Myself. I have power to lay it down, and I have power to take it again.** This command I have received from My Father (John 10:18; emphasis added).

Jesus is saying, in effect, that He will *resurrect Himself!* Talk about a miraculous feat! It's one thing to resurrect someone else, but to resurrect *Himself* is a powerful miracle indeed!

Blessed Assurance

So, how can we know whether we have committed the unpardonable sin? Well, we must return to the source of this declaration to get its context before we can answer this fully.

As already quoted from Matthew 12:26-32 (see page 131), Jesus was responding to the claim by the Pharisees and others that He was able to cast out demons because of the cooperation of Beelzebub (a.k.a. Satan). Since it was obvious that Jesus was exorcising demons by the power of the Spirit of God (Matthew 12:28), it was not only preposterous to claim that Satan would cooperate in his own defeat, but Jesus says it is blasphemous (an insult) to the Holy Spirit of God to attribute the Holy Spirit's work to the Devil. Furthermore, since the sons of these bystanders were apparently also able to exorcise demons, Jesus asked who they thought had empowered their own sons to cast out demons (Matthew 12:27).

Just as Nicodemus recognized the power of God emanating from Jesus (John 3:1-2)–and Nicodemus was also a Pharisee, per John 3:1–these other Pharisees had to admit the same thing. Interestingly, Nicodemus said, "**We** know . . ." (emphasis added). However, it was their utter frustration over not being able to exercise any control over Jesus that prompted them to be so blasphemous. As the Apostle John reported later, near the end of Jesus' earthly ministry, "The Pharisees therefore said among themselves, 'You see that you are accomplishing nothing. Look, the world has gone after Him!'" (John 12:19). Just prior to that, they had convened a council meeting immediately after Jesus had raised His friend Lazarus from the dead to discuss what to do about Jesus' influence over the people. Here's what transpired:

> Then the chief priests and the Pharisees gathered a council and said, "What shall we do? For this Man works many signs. If we let Him alone like this, everyone will believe in Him, and the Romans will come and take away both our place and nation." And one of them, Caiaphas, being high priest that year, said to them, "You know nothing at all, nor do you consider that it is expedient for us that one man should die for the people, and not that the whole nation should perish." Now this he did not say on his own authority; but being high priest

that year he prophesied that Jesus would die for the nation, and not for that nation only, but also that He would gather together in one the children of God who were scattered abroad. Then, from that day on, they plotted to put Him to death (John 11:47-53).

It appears they were more concerned about their own political influence than they were about being right in their assessment of who Jesus was. They were blinded by their evil ambition to maintain control over the people of Israel at any cost. As Jesus told them on another occasion,

> If I do not do the works of My Father, do not believe Me; but if I do, though you do not believe Me, believe the works, that you may know and believe that the Father is in Me, and I in Him (John 10:37-38).

This is the primary reason Jesus performed His deeds of power. It was to be a witness to the people—both the leaders and the citizens—that the Messiah had truly come, because no one else in all their history had ever done as many mighty deeds as Jesus had done. How else would He have been able to do all these things? As one of His healed witnesses testified to them in John 9:1-34):

> Now we know that God does not hear sinners; but if anyone is a worshiper of God and does His will, He hears him. Since the world began it has been unheard of that anyone opened the eyes of one who was born blind. **If this Man were not from God, He could do nothing** (John 9:31-33; emphasis added).

We can ascertain from all this, then, that there really was no excuse for these self-righteous Pharisees to deny that Jesus truly was the long-awaited Messiah. God made it perfectly clear to everyone, including them. It was therefore a matter of accepting the obvious truth or rejecting it. It was the pinnacle of wickedness to accuse Jesus of consorting with the Devil to deceive the people into believing He was the Messiah. The old saying that "there are none so blind as those who will not see" is most apropos here. Only those who *willfully* choose to turn a blind eye to the truth can be so brazen as to attribute the obvious work of God's Holy Spirit to Satan. It is, therefore, *a cognizant, willful act,* and that is possibly God's reason for refusing to forgive it.

By cognizant, I mean that the violator is fully knowledgeable and aware of what he or she is doing and saying when he or she commits this sin. It is therefore not a sin one commits ignorantly or unintentionally. Thus, if you look upon an obvious work of God, such as the exorcism of one or more demons from a person, and then with clear knowledge and understanding you brazenly attribute the glory for this work to Satan instead of God, you have committed the unpardonable sin. Only an arrogant, resistant, defiant person will commit such a sin. Someone like these self-righteous Pharisees, who saw themselves as better than and above everyone else in all of Israel (including the very Son of God Himself, Jesus Christ) is the sort of person who would commit such a sin. In fact, it was their commission of this sin which prompted Jesus to make this pronouncement concerning the unpardonable sin in the first place.

As the Scripture plainly says in more than one place: "God resists the proud, but gives grace to the humble" (Proverbs 3:34; James 4:6; and 1 Peter 5:5). So, if you want to receive grace from God, you must relinquish your pride, humble yourself before Him, and turn from your wicked ways, *even* if you call yourself a Christian or a child of God. Compare 2 Chronicles 7:14 and 1 Peter 5:6, which are directed straight at the people of God.

Failure to humble oneself before God will result in His judgment rather than His gracious forgiveness. Indeed, the person who remains humble before God and his or her fellow human beings will *never* have to fear the possibility of committing the unpardonable sin, because this particular sin *cannot* be committed by a humble person. It is of necessity a sin of pride.

We will discuss more about God's divine judgment in Chapter 9, but first, we must cover the catastrophe of apostasy, which is the subject of the next chapter. What *is* the catastrophe of apostasy, and how can we avoid it? Keep reading to find out.

CHAPTER EIGHT: THE CATASTROPHE OF APOSTASY

In the first edition of this book, I completely overlooked and omitted the importance of warning the reader about the supreme catastrophe of apostasy. For several years now, I have been very desirous of writing this second edition for the express purpose of correcting that omission by including an explanation of this terrible danger to the soul. Indeed, the previous edition's discussion about the salvation of the LORD was flatly incomplete without it. Therefore, in this chapter, I hope to lay out in detail what apostasy is, understanding how it can happen, avoiding it, why it is often disputed, and what to do if you, or someone you know, is drifting toward it. So, without further delay, let us proceed.

Defining Apostasy

The English word *apostasy* comes from the Greek word *apostasia* (pronounced ah-pahs-tah-SEE-yah; Strong's G646; ἀποστασία),[38] which, according to Thayer, literally means "a falling away, defection, apostasy."[39] In the common use of the word, it means to defect from a former philosophical or religious belief. Merriam-Webster's Online Dictionary defines it this way: "1 : an act of refusing to continue to follow, obey, or recognize a religious faith" and "2 : abandonment of a previous loyalty : DE-FECTION"[40] Therefore, to be an apostate from the true Christian faith, one must have abandoned his or her past trust in the biblical teachings of and about Jesus Christ in *The Holy Bible*. *How,* pray tell—and *why*—would such a thing happen with a genuine Christian believer? Those are very good questions, so let's consider them now.

Understanding How Apostasy Happens

Firstly, to become an apostate from *any* belief, one must have been a sincere believer, because one simply cannot abandon a faith if he or she never had it. Furthermore, since abandoning faith in a *false* statement of belief is technically apostasy, too (whether it was an erroneous belief about the One True God or whether it was belief in another *false* god), deserting that *false* faith for the *true* faith is *not* the same thing in the mind of the One True God as apostatizing from *true* faith in Jesus Christ. From the biblical perspective, switching from a false belief to the true belief is *repentance from the sin of idolatry* to true faith in God's Plan of Salvation: Jesus Christ and His work upon the cross.

So, we return now to our original question: how could a genuine Christian believer become an apostate? Well, one can become an *unbeliever* in the same way he or she became a *believer* in Christ initially—*by faith*, or, as in the case of apostasy, by *losing*

faith, abandoning faith or by *reappropriating faith* into someone or something else. In other words, he or she would simply
choose to place his or her faith into something else besides the
biblical teaching about Christ. According to the Apostle Paul, we
are truly saved by placing our faith in God's grace, *not* by *earning*
God's favor in *any* way:

> **For by grace you have been saved through faith,**
> and that not of yourselves; *it is* the gift of God, not of
> works, lest anyone should boast (Ephesians 2:8-9; em-
> phasis added).

Therefore, since we are saved through faith *in* God's grace, we
may also apostatize through reappropriating faith *from* God's
grace. This happens when a professing Christian decides to
switch to something like Islam or Buddhism or New Ageism, but
it also occurs when a professing Christian decides to embrace
atheism, agnosticism or universalism and the various views asso-
ciated with those mindsets.

During my lifetime, which includes approximately three decades of service as both a pastor and an Army Chaplain, I have con-
versed with numerous individuals who informed me they had
formerly been Christians but had somehow decided they preferred
another belief system. My first encounter was with a young woman
at the university I attended while serving as a student pastor in my
first pastoral appointment. She had renounced her former faith in
Christ and had no interest in reconsidering. A few years later, while
I attended seminary, I participated in an institutional ministry

program and visited regularly with a man in a long-term care facility who was in his eighties. He told me he had been a believer in his younger years, but he was by then an atheist. Years later, while serving on active duty in the Army, I talked with an enlisted soldier who said he had been raised as a believer in a Presbyterian Christian home, but he now embraced Wicca. Several years after that, I attended a military Chaplain course with a Chaplain who said he had converted from being a Lutheran minister to being an Islamic Imam, and he expressed a personal debt of gratitude to the Roman Catholic priest who had encouraged him to make the switch. After completing that Army Chaplain course, I returned to my assigned duty station and served with another Army officer who said he had been raised in a Christian home, but he had decided he was then an atheist.

Although I didn't attempt to dissuade the Army Chaplain, nothing I said to the others made any difference in their thinking. I am inclined to believe it is because God had given them over to what they had chosen. The Holy Spirit was no longer calling them to return to Christ. They had settled on apostasy, so God had let them have their way.

Avoiding Apostasy

Transitioning from faith to apostasy can occur gradually over a long span of time, or it can occur rapidly over a short span of time. For instance, a believer may allow a series of unbelievers' challenges to the veracity of his or her faith to go unsettled in his or her mind for a while until he or she gradually begins to lose faith in what was previously believed. This often happens within one's own unbelieving family or through the relationship with a highly treasured, but unbelieving, friend, if the new believer does not guard against it. In any case, God wants us to consider *His* Word (as found in the Bible) above *everyone else's* words. Furthermore, He wants us to sever ties with those who would, through their own stubborn rejection of Christ, make shipwreck of our faith, *even* if they are our family and dearest friends. Jesus makes this point particularly clear in Luke's Gospel, as quoted below:

> "Do you suppose that I came to grant peace on earth? I tell you, no, but rather division; for from now on five *members* in one household will be divided, three against two and two against three. They will be divided, father against son and son against father, mother against daughter and daughter against mother, mother-in-law against daughter-in-law and daughter-in-law against mother-in-law" (Luke 12:51-53 NASB; compare with Matthew 10:34-36).

> "If anyone comes to Me, and does not hate his own father and mother and wife and children and brothers and sisters, yes, and even his own life, he cannot be My disciple" (Luke 14:26 NASB; compare with Matthew 10:37-38).

What Jesus means in each of these passages is that believers must choose Him and His Kingdom over everyone and everything else in this world, including our own life. Neither beloved relatives nor friends nor the threat of losing our life should be more important to us, or else Jesus will consider that to be a denial and rejection of Him. Consider this: if Jesus was willing to sacrifice His own life on the cross for the world, why would we be unwilling to make the same sort of sacrifice for *His* sake?

Conversely, a believer may experience a severe emotional trauma from a tragedy in life, such as the death of a beloved person or the loss of a beloved object or dream, that causes him or her to doubt God's love, or even His existence, and consequently abandon faith in God altogether. This is especially true when the believer earnestly interceded to God, yet God did not grant his or her petition. In either of these instances, God may be testing a believer's faith to prompt him or her to seek in God's Word (the Bible) the answers to these challenges by unbelievers, which will ultimately lead the believer into a deeper relationship with and understanding of God. In the second case, God may be confronting the believer with keeping his or her affections properly prioritized with Christ (who *is God*, after all) at the very top of the list.

I say, "God *may* be testing a believer's faith" or confronting a believer's priorities in these cases, because there may be other reasons why we experience these sorts of trials, too. My book *Seven Keys to Effective Prayer* deals with only a few of the reasons why God may not grant our petitions. In that book, I explain how living righteously, having faith in God, forgiving, abiding in Christ, honoring your spouse, living in unity with believers, and delighting in the Lord can open the channels of communication between God and us and qualify us to receive His blessings, including the granting of our petitions to Him that agree with His divine will. We should understand, therefore, that God will not grant those petitions that contradict His divine will, as we learn from a reading of the Apostle John's first letter:

> This is the confidence which we have before Him, that, **if we ask anything according to His will, He hears us** (1 John 5:14 NASB; emphasis added).

This may be one of the most frequent causes of apostasy in those believers who think that God will grant them anything they ask, only to learn that God will indeed deny those petitions which contradict His will for His people. A truly committed and submitted believer will, however, accept whatever God *disallows,* as well as what He grants.

I think Jesus' explanation of His Parable of the Sower is fitting here. In this parable, Jesus is describing people who accepted and believed God's Word initially, but then faltered in the face of life's troubles, perhaps because they expected God to protect them from all such troubles. Reconsider Jesus' explanation of that parable now with this understanding:

> "Now the parable is this: The seed is the word of God. The ones along the path are those who have heard; then the devil comes and takes away the word from their hearts, so that they may not believe and be saved. And the ones on the rock are those who, when they hear the word, receive it with joy. But these have no root; **they believe for a while, and in time of testing fall away.** And as for what fell among the thorns, they are those who hear, but **as they go on their way they are choked by the cares and riches and pleasures of life, and their fruit does not mature.** As for that in

the good soil, they are those who, hearing the word, hold
it fast in an honest and good heart, and bear fruit with
patience" (Luke 8:11-15 ESV; emphasis added).

The Greek word that is translated as "fall away" in this passage is *aphistemi* (pronounced af-ISS-tay-mee; Strong's G868;
ἀφίστημι),[41] and it is one of several Greek words that describe
the concepts of withdrawal, abandon, departure, revolt, faithless
and apostasy. Anyone who argues that no true believer can apostatize should take it up with Jesus, because He is clearly saying
here that those with hearts like stony soil ". . . believe for a while,
and in time of testing fall away" (Luke 8:13 ESV). Furthermore,
why would God warn us as He does in the following Scripture?

> Take care, brethren, that there not be in any one of you
> an evil, unbelieving heart that falls away from the living
> God (Hebrews 3:12 NASB).

Firstly, the Scripture writer refers to the recipients of his letter
as "brethren," signifying their spiritual connection in the faith.
Secondly, he writes to be careful "that there not be in any one of
you [emphasis added] an evil, unbelieving heart that falls away
from the living God." There's simply no denying that God is warning us as true believers to be on guard against doubt and unbelief,
which can easily lead us into the catastrophe of apostasy.

So, now that we understand better *how* a true believer may
become an apostate, let us consider the next question of *why* a
believer might apostatize, which requires a bit more thought. To
keep it as simple and concise as possible, however, I believe it

can be the result of one of two things: 1) being disappointed by God—i.e., not getting what we expect from God, and 2) failing to grow closer in our relationship with Jesus after we initially place our faith in Him for salvation. The first result, however, can usually be eliminated by overcoming the second.

Lack of closeness through knowledge and understanding is also essentially how a divorce happens between a husband and wife—they either fail to grow closer together through getting to know and understand each other following their wedding day, or they slowly drift apart while navigating the trials and troubles of living in this fallen world. They may develop a very intimate and meaningful relationship for the first several months of their marriage, but after beginning to pursue a career and adding a child or more to their family, they will begin to drift apart as they allow other priorities to interfere with the ongoing development of their relationship. Failure to forgive past grievances and/or failure to keep the fires of romance burning will doom *any* marriage either to cold indifference (where the couple simply stays together for their children's sake or for their religious convictions) or to painful divorce (where they put their own interests above those of the family and likely repeat the pattern in their next marriage). Certainly, there may be several other contributing factors, but the root cause of drifting apart and divorce is ultimately failure to maintain optimal intimacy through mutual love, respect, knowledge and understanding of each other in the relationship.

This same problem can occur in our relationship with Jesus if we do not prioritize spending time with Him through daily prayer and Scripture study, and then strive to apply what we learn from our time spent in the Scriptures. Allowing other priorities to usurp Jesus' rightful place as *first* in our hearts and lives *can* lead to apostasy if we do not change course. While it is not a foregone conclusion that everyone who drifts away from Christ will apostatize, it is most definitely a dangerous risk that one is taking, as Jesus warns in His letters to the seven churches of Asia Minor (read Revelation 1:20-3:22). Among them, only the churches of Smyrna and Philadelphia received no warnings to repent.

Disputing the Doctrine of Apostasy

There is a sizable group of professing Christians who, unfortunately, discount the doctrine of apostasy altogether, or else they dilute it to such a degree that it is no longer truly apostasy according to its classic definition. Perhaps this is because they simply can't accept the prospect that it is possible for one to forfeit his or her salvation. Pay special attention that I used the word "forfeit" here and not the word "lose." A sincere believer in Christ Jesus cannot *lose* his or her salvation, as if it is either misplaced or stolen (for it **cannot** be stolen; see John 10:27-30), but he or she *can forfeit* that salvation by becoming an apostate. When we forfeit something, whether it is a game or a piece of property or something else, we willingly relinquish it. It is not, and indeed it *cannot*, be taken from us by force, because that would not fit the definition of forfeiture. Such a forceful removal of what belongs to us would be called *theft*, not forfeiture. Therefore, we cannot be robbed of our salvation, either by Satan or by one of his evil minions (whether demonic or human), which is what Jesus was truly teaching us in John 10:27-30. However, if we change our mind about Christ, about the truth of the Bible, or about any of the understanding we have from the Bible about God and His salvation of our soul, then we *can willingly* lay aside what we once believed and become an apostate.

While apostasy may not be a sin from which one cannot repent in every case (contrast Ezekiel 33:11 & Hosea 14:4 with Hebrews 6:4-6), it remains a sin which, like *all* sin, separates God's people from God—*until* they repent. However, if an apostate is unwilling to return to his or her former faith in Christ after both gentle nudging and firm prodding with Scriptural applications and brotherly or sisterly confrontation, this is a strong indication that God is not prompting him or her and has probably given him or her over to this decision (as with those named in Romans 1:28). If God does not call us unto Christ by His Holy Spirit, we are helpless and hopeless, because Jesus says we will *never* come to Him on our own (see John 6:44). All we can do then is pray, unless God commands us *not* to pray (see 1 John 5:14-16).

Like the sin of blaspheming the Holy Spirit (explained in Chapter 7), apostasy is not an inadvertent act of ignorance or oversight, because to abandon one's faith, one must make a *conscious choice* to discontinue believing. Whether this choice occurs after an extended period of gradual loss of faith (by which the believer finally concludes he or she no longer believes), or whether it occurs in a moment of extreme duress after a shocking trauma (by which the believer suddenly decides his or her former faith has been in vain), it is a deliberate *choice,* nonetheless.

If one tries to argue that such a person was never a true believing Christian in the first place, he or she is making a judgment about something that only the One True God can know, i.e., the full contents and true intents of a human heart. As the prophet Jeremiah wrote:

> "The heart *is* deceitful above all *things,* And desperately wicked; Who can know it? **I, the LORD, search the heart, *I* test the mind, Even to give every man according to his ways, According to the fruit of his doings**" (Jeremiah 17:9-10; emphasis added).

To argue that such a person did not understand what he or she was doing when he or she made a profession of faith in Jesus Christ as Lord and Savior and was therefore never really saved is also quite presumptive, because the apostatizing person understands enough about what he or she is doing to believe that he or she now prefers an alternate belief system to that which he or she formerly believed from *The Holy Bible.* Those who try to make their case using these arguments are only grasping at the wind to avoid a very unpleasant reality: that God will indeed reject someone who, despite a previous profession of faith in His Plan of Salvation, has now rejected Him and His Plan. So, as unfathomable as it is, and as disturbing as it is, that's how a genuine believer could and would become an apostate.

To say that no truly saved believer would do such a thing is ignoring all the references in the Bible to the existence of apostasy among the people of Israel, God's chosen people. Can you hear the urgency in God's tone as He speaks to His rebellious people through the prophet Ezekiel?

> Say to them: '*As* I live,' says the Lord GOD, 'I have no pleasure in the death of the wicked, but that the wicked turn from his way and live. **Turn, turn from your evil ways! For why should you die, O house of Israel?**' (Ezekiel 33:11; emphasis added).

The warning in Ezekiel 33:12-13 is even *more* concerning. Here, God warns that a righteous man who begins to think that, because he has been approved as righteous, he can now afford to be wicked, will *not* be saved.

> "Therefore you, O son of man, say to the children of your people: 'The righteousness of the righteous man shall not deliver him in the day of his transgression; as for the wickedness of the wicked, he shall not fall because of it in the day that he turns from his wickedness; nor shall the righteous be able to live because of *his righteousness* in the day that he sins.' **When I say to the righteous *that* he shall surely live, but he trusts in his own righteousness and commits iniquity, none of his righteous works shall be remembered; but because of the iniquity that he has committed, he shall die**" (Ezekiel 33:12-13; see also Ezekiel 3:17-21; emphasis added).

When God says "die" in this passage, He is referring to the second death, as reported in Revelation 20:6 & 14. How much clearer can God make it?

This sort of thinking referenced in Ezekiel 33:13 sounds to me a lot like today's hyper grace movement, where we hear preachers and teachers informing believers that, as Christians, we are now under grace and not under the Law of the Old Testament (see Romans 6:14), so we don't have to abide by *any* of it, including the Ten Commandments, because Jesus has fulfilled *all* the Law (see Matthew 5:17). This teaching is a perversion of what the Scriptures are really saying. It is true that Jesus has kept the Law in its entirety (something none of us can ever do), but a more careful reading of Matthew 5:17 demonstrates that Jesus did not *destroy* the Law, or do away with it, but rather He kept it without sinning even once (see Hebrews 4:15), so that He could be the perfect and sinless, atoning sacrifice for all of humanity.

It is also true that Christians live under grace and not under the Law, but even so, we are *not* supposed to let sin have dominion over us. Re-read Romans 6:14 and pay close attention to the first half of that passage, then go all the way back to Genesis and read very carefully what God says to Cain *before* Cain killed his brother:

> "If you do well, will you not be accepted? And if you do not do well, **sin lies at the door. And its desire *is* for you, but you should rule over it.**" (Genesis 4:7; emphasis added).

Way back before the Law of Moses even existed, God was cautioning Cain that he must rule over sin in his life! I wonder: could this be what Jesus was referring to when He prophesied that He will dismiss the lawless hypocrites from His presence on the day of judgment? Read Jesus' own words:

> "Not everyone who says to Me, 'Lord, Lord,' shall enter the kingdom of heaven, but he who does the will of My Father in heaven. Many will say to Me in that day, 'Lord, Lord, have we not prophesied in Your name, cast out demons in Your name, and done many wonders in Your name?' And then I will declare to them, 'I never knew you; **depart from Me, you who practice lawlessness!**'" (Matthew 7:21-23; emphasis added).

Maybe Jesus is referring to formerly righteous believers here who are trusting in their righteousness (that they are under grace and not under the Law), so that they think they can now live lawlessly.

I cannot tell you how many times I've argued about the doctrine of apostasy with those who dispute it, and they say, "Such a person was never truly saved in the first place!" Consider this: we coach new converts to Christ to pray "the sinner's prayer" after us, word-for-word, and never even doubt their sincerity or the efficacy of their salvation when they do, so why are we so swift to doubt their sincerity or the efficacy of that initial salvation experience when they later decide to apostatize? First, since only God can know the true intents of a human heart, who are we to judge another's sincerity in committing to the Lord or the surety of his or her salvation? Second, you would never try to make that argument *before* the person apostatized, so why would you try to make it *afterward*? My friend, if you take the position of denying apostasy, you are negating the very eternal security that you are trying to protect, because this means that *you* have no way of knowing whether *you* are truly saved, since you have no idea what your future holds and whether you, too, might one day reject Christ based on a severe trial and subsequent lapse of your faith!

I know you believe you are absolute in your certainty that you will *never* leave or deny Christ, but don't forget that the Apostle Peter was sure that he would never leave or deny Christ, too, and so were the other disciples who were with him and Jesus in the Upper Room that night of Jesus' Last Supper with them (see Matthew 26:31-35). However, we know from each of the Gospel accounts that *all* the disciples did indeed scatter and leave Jesus, though Peter and John managed to compose themselves enough to follow Jesus and His captors at a distance and even enter Annas' home (who was, apparently, the former high priest now living in retirement; see John 18:15-16). Furthermore, Peter *did* deny Jesus later that same night, just as Jesus prophesied that he would (see Matthew 26:69-75).

You see, because we can't know the future (unless God reveals it to us) we can *never* say with any degree of certainty what we will or will not do or what will or will not happen to us. Jesus gave Peter a hint of what was coming, but Peter did not believe it.

And the Lord said, "Simon, Simon! Indeed, Satan has asked for you, that he may sift *you* as wheat. But I have prayed for you, that your faith should not fail; and when you have returned to *Me,* strengthen your brethren." But he said to Him, "Lord, I am ready to go with You, both to prison and to death." Then He said, "I tell you, Peter, the rooster shall not crow this day before you will deny three times that you know Me" (Luke 22:31-34).

Notice that Jesus did not say that Satan could *not* have Peter to sift him like wheat—only that Jesus had prayed that Peter's faith might not fail. Even so, Jesus already knew that Peter would return afterwards (see verse 32 in that passage). There-fore, this does not appear to be a case of apostasy by Peter as much as it was a fearful act of self-preservation, but what might have happened if Jesus had not prayed for Peter's faith not to fail? Only God knows.

So, how can we be certain of our salvation by Christ if we can't know our future? That's easy. Since we *obtain* our salva-tion *through faith* in what Jesus has done for us, we *maintain* our salvation *through faith* in what Jesus has done for us. So long as we do not abandon faith in what the entire Bible tells us that Jesus Christ has done for us, we *cannot lose,* and we *will not forfeit,* our salvation. It's just that simple!

Due to the refusal by many Christians to accept the doctrine of apostasy, it has been hotly debated for centuries, especially among those who hold to the erroneously defined Calvinist doc-trine of eternal security. While we can consult commentaries written about the Bible by learned men of history for clarification and confirmation of biblical doctrines, we must exercise extreme caution not to adopt any teachings from these sources which either subtly contradict or overtly dispute the plain teachings of the Bible. Therefore, if we rely solely upon the Bible for our doctrinal instruction and not upon the interpretation and commentary of mere mortal men, such as Calvin or Luther or me or anyone else outside the group of divinely inspired men of the Scriptures, then we can rest assured we are not being led astray by false doctrine.

There are several other references in the Scriptures to the deadly danger of apostasy, such as the entire epistle to the Galatians, which was authored by the Apostle Paul for the very purpose of countering the teaching of salvation by any other means than grace through faith in Jesus Christ's atoning crucifixion and resurrection (see Galatians 1:6-9; 2:21; & especially 5:4-6). To further assist you in identifying and avoiding apostasy, I strongly recommend you obtain a copy of *Nave's Topical Bible* and look up the word "apostasy" in it for numerous other Scripture references regarding apostasy. You can get it for free when you download and install the Bible software e-Sword, to which I give my highest recommendation.[42]

What Can We Do to Counteract Apostasy?

This brings us to our final point to consider in this chapter about the doctrine of apostasy: what can we do if we realize that we are, or if someone we love is, drifting into apostasy? The strongest antidote for apostasy is a combination of repentance and faith. We repent by turning back to the Lord from whatever has lured us away from Him, but how do we strengthen our faith when it appears to be waning? The Apostle Paul gives us the answer:

> So then faith *comes* by hearing, and hearing by the word of God (Romans 10:17).

Therefore, the best thing you can do if you feel that your faith is failing is to read God's Word, *The Holy Bible,* or to listen to it on CD or some other medium, as much as you can. It will give you hope and encouragement and strength to continue during your challenging times. Reading what God has already done for other believers and what He promises to do for us will bring great comfort and encouragement to carry on. Also, reading God's Word will give us insight and understanding about spiritual matters that we were either previously ignorant of or that we have forgotten.

If you notice a loved one who appears to be drifting toward apostasy, urge him or her to repent and follow this same plan of Bible reading and study as soon as possible. However, while it's hard enough to motivate ourselves to enact disciplinary steps, it can be even harder to motivate someone else to take these same steps, because we have no control over another's decisions or actions. If you truly love your relative or friend, however, you will not make it easy for him or her to put you off or push you away. Keep urging until you break through, although if one becomes belligerent in resistance, you may cause more harm than good. In that case, it's best to try and enlist the help of someone else who may have more success than you, because you may be too close to the situation. If you find yourself cut-off from the relationship, though, your only recourse may be persistent and fervent prayer. If you succeed in turning back a stray, however, the Apostle James says:

> Brethren, if anyone among you wanders from the truth, and someone turns him back, let him know that **he who turns a sinner from the error of his way will save a soul from death and cover a multitude of sins** (James 5:19-20; emphasis added).

What further Scriptural proof of the doctrine of apostasy could we denote than those words? For one cannot "wander from the truth" and be turned back to it unless he or she had first believed and accepted it as truth. Furthermore, what better segue could we find than this to transition into our next chapter's discussion about The Judgment? So, how *do* we escape the judgment? Keep reading to find out.

CHAPTER NINE: THE JUDGMENT

Everyone wants to believe in the love, mercy, and grace of God, but no one wants to accept or believe that God also has a judgmental side to His character. This judgmental side of God's character comes out of His divine righteousness, which *requires* the application of justice. In other words, God *cannot* be righteous if He allows wrongdoing to go unpunished. Therefore, He chose to come into the world as a human being to satisfy the demand of His own Law.

Ironically, when judging matters of right and wrong and restitution, we human beings want justice for everybody else but mercy and grace for ourselves. Though somewhat humorous, this is definitely no laughing matter.

Divine Justice

When I say there is a judgmental side to God's character, I mean that God must *necessarily* pronounce judgment on those who ignore (and thereby disobey) His righteous Word, which is synonymous with His commandments and Law, even though He usually delays executing justice on any case level to allow the sinner(s) time to confess, repent, and ask for mercy, grace and pardon. The only way to escape the *final* judgment for sin, however, is to enter the New Covenant God has enacted for us. Thus, for God to indifferently overlook disobedience to His Word–collectively known as sin–would make Him unjust.

Failure to accept and comply with the terms of God's covenant will leave one *outside* God's covenant and subject to the righteous demands of God's Law. Fulfilling the requirement for the judgment of sin is why God designed the means of justification for repentant sinners that we now call the Plan of Salvation, by which He *personally* came into the world as a human being (whom we know as Jesus) to live the sinless life that none of us is capable of living, to substitute Himself for us in the punishment for our sin, and to use His sinless blood as an atonement (covering) for *all* human sin–from Adam and Eve to whoever will be the last person born on earth. Yes, that includes such wicked people in history as Nimrod, Nero, Genghis Khan, Adolf Hitler, and Saddam Hussein, just to name a few. Since sin had to be judged and punished (because of divine justice), God resolved to satisfy these requirements by substituting *Himself* for fallen, sinful humanity.

This once-and-for-all atonement for sin does not therefore license the brazen practice of sin or even the occasional flagrant violation of God's commandments under the guise of being "not under law but under grace" (Romans 6:14). It is intended for the satisfaction of God's Law regarding the everlasting damnation and punishment that must be meted out to the unjustified sinner.

An unjustified sinner is a sinner who is outside God's covenant for salvation. This means that to be justified and saved by God, one must not only repent of practicing a sinful lifestyle but also accept and enter God's covenant for salvation. So, even if one repents of a sinful lifestyle (such as leaving prostitution, getting clean from drugs and/or alcohol addiction or ceasing thievery, lying, fornication, adultery, or murder), if such a one does not also enter God's covenant by accepting His offer of atonement, justification, and salvation made possible by Jesus through His death and resurrection, such a one is still condemned to Hell for being an *unjustified* sinner. For that matter, even if one has lived a relatively good and moral life (whether he or she grew up in a Christian home or not), without entering this covenant with God, such a one is still condemned to Hell for being an *unjustified* sinner.

An *unrepentant* sinner, on the other hand, is one who *continues* to practice sin as a lifestyle rather than turn away from it, even if he or she also claims to have entered God's covenant. If such a person thinks he has saved his soul from damnation by the mere saying of a formulaic prayer of repentance, yet continues unabated and unrepentant in the practice of sin, this person is greatly deceived, because where there is no repentance from sin, there is no conversion of the heart and soul, and where there is no conversion of the heart and soul, there is no forgiveness, justification, or salvation of the soul from sin (compare Luke 3:3-9 and Acts 26:19-20).

Furthermore, just saying we're sorry for our sin is not the same thing as repenting from our sin either, because the word *repent* means *to turn away from* something. Thus, to repent of our sin means that we turn away from practicing sin as a *lifestyle*. It does not mean that we won't occasionally fail in our goal of avoiding sin after accepting Jesus' atonement for our collective sins, but rather it means that we are struggling with all our strength *not* to yield to temptations to commit sin. Once we accept Christ's atoning sacrifice for our sins and repent (turn away from) our former sins, He justifies us, marks us as His by giving us His Holy Spirit, and calls us to a life of righteousness ever after.

Getting Right with God

Justification is a fancy word for "made right" or "declared righteous." Since none of us could ever atone for even *one* of our *own* sins, let alone the sins of anyone else, we could never authoritatively make or declare *ourselves or anyone else* righteous. This is something only God can do, because only God is eternally righteous as both the Creator God and the God-Man–Jesus. Until we understand and accept our *inability* to live righteously enough to meet God's standard of righteousness, until we accept Jesus as the substitutionary sacrifice for *all* our sins, and until we cease trying to measure up to God's standard of righteousness *on our own*, we will remain outside His covenant with *no hope of salvation*. That ought to be a sobering thought for any of us to consider, but alas, too many people–whether church-going or not–continue to strive in the flesh to do what is impossible for any sinful human being to do: that is, to be good enough for God to accept into His holy Kingdom.

According to the Apostle Paul, this is the very reason God gave the Law to Israel in the first place, not to make anyone righteous before God, but to demonstrate the utter futility and hopelessness of trying to live righteously *enough* to be accepted by God. In fact, it was after Israel's first up-close-and-personal visitation from God when He gave the Law to them on Mt. Sinai that they developed a great dread of ever experiencing such a close encounter again. The account is recorded in Exodus, chapters 19 and 20.

Before the divine visitation, God separated them out as a people unto Himself and said:

> "'You have seen what I did to the Egyptians, and *how* I bore you on eagles' wings and brought you to Myself. Now therefore, if you will indeed obey My voice and keep My covenant, then you shall be a special treasure to Me above all people; for all the earth *is* Mine. And you shall be to Me a kingdom of priests and a holy nation'" (Exodus 19:4-6).

Next, they eagerly proclaimed, ". . . 'All that the LORD has spoken we will do' . . ." (Exodus 19:8). After God appeared to them on Mt. Sinai, however, the experience was so terrifying that the leaders of Israel called upon Moses to be their liaison ever after. Moses recorded it thusly:

> Now all the people witnessed the thunderings, the lightning flashes, the sound of the trumpet, and the mountain

smoking; and when the people saw *it,* they trembled and stood afar off. Then they said to Moses, 'You speak with us, and we will hear; but let not God speak with us, lest we die.' **And Moses said to the people, 'Do not fear; for God has come to test you, and that His fear may be before you, so that you may not sin'** (Exodus 20:18-20; emphasis added).

This pronouncement from the elders of Israel came immediately after God had spoken to them the Ten Commandments, and they repeated it twice more after God had given them even *more* commandments in Exodus 20:22-24:18 (see Exodus 24:3 & 7, specifically). However, as we learn several chapters later (which, according to Exodus 24:18, covers a period of forty days and nights), they soon forgot both God's commandments *and* their pledge of "All that the LORD has spoken we will do." Beginning with the description in Exodus 32:1, they apparently broke *at least* the first two or three of the Ten Commandments *at once* within hours of sculpting a golden calf idol. The Israelites were out of Egypt, but getting Egypt out of the Israelites would be another matter indeed!

It is precisely this propensity towards sin that God wanted to address in His people. He had already warned Cain in Genesis 4:7 of the danger of sin lying in wait for him and the imperative that he must master it, and that was before there were even any Ten Commandments! The Apostle Paul wrote something similar in his letter to the Romans: "For **sin shall not have dominion over you,** for you are not under law but under grace" Romans 6:14; emphasis added). With all the focus on being "under grace" rather than "under law," too many Christians have completely missed the imperative not to allow sin to have dominion over them. Why would God issue such a commandment both to Cain (Genesis 4:7) and to Christian believers (Romans 6:14) if resisting and mastering sin is impossible? The answer is: He *wouldn't,* of course!

The Apostle Peter even went so far as to say:

> Therefore, brethren, be even more diligent to make your call and election sure, for **if you do these things you will never stumble [that is, sin];** for so an entrance will be supplied to you abundantly into the everlasting kingdom of our Lord and Savior Jesus Christ (2 Peter 1:10-11; emphasis added).

The Greek word which is translated as *stumble* here is *ptaio* (pronounced PTAH-yo; Strong's G4417; πταίω).[43] It literally means to trip or stumble, and it is a figurative way of saying, "to commit sin."

The Purpose of the Law

Now, getting back to Paul's instruction about the purpose of the Law in his letter to the church in Rome, he wrote:

> Moreover **the law entered that the offense might abound.** But where sin abounded, grace abounded much more . . . (Romans 5:20; emphasis added).

This means that the law was given to raise our consciousness of sin so that the need for mercy and pardon would become apparent and the grace of God could be applied when requested. As Paul wrote a couple of chapters later in his letter to the Romans:

What shall we say then? *Is* the law sin? Certainly not! On the contrary, **I would not have known sin except through the law. For I would not have known covetousness unless the law had said, 'YOU SHALL NOT COVET.' But sin, taking opportunity by the commandment, produced in me all *manner of evil desire.*** For apart from the law sin *was* dead (Romans 7:7-8; emphasis added).

We see then that the Law of God is not the problem; *sin* is the problem. God's Law simply makes clear how *much* of a problem sin really is! In fact, like a mirror which we hold before our face to realize just how dirty and disheveled our facial appearance is, the Law reveals just how *unrighteous* we are and how much in need of repentance, forgiveness, and cleansing from sin we truly are. Once we reach that point in our understanding, the Law will have done its work to make us aware of our need. We can then call upon God for His merciful pardon and His gracious enrollment in His Heavenly Kingdom. I'll write more about this Heavenly Kingdom in the next chapter.

Of course, the problem is getting most people to *realize* their need for pardon and salvation. Until they come to this realization, they resist the notion that they need either pardon *or* salvation. Many of the folks who are headed for God's judgment reject any idea that such a thing as divine judgment even exists. Others headed for God's judgment simply misunderstand how to escape it in the first place.

In any case, as I understand it, all people who are presently headed for divine judgment fall into one of three main categories:

1) those who reject the existence of God (atheists); 2) those who doubt the existence of God (agnostics); and 3) those who have the wrong concept of the One True God. This third category is where most people on earth are classified, because it includes not only people from non-Christian religions but many within *supposed* Christian faith groups as well. In fact, many of the people with the wrong concept of the One True God sit on church pews of Christian orthodoxy every Sunday, week after week, thinking they're okay because of where they're sitting or what they're doing, rather than being gravely concerned about what they believe and in whom they must trust. Having the correct concept of the One True God is essential for the salvation of one's eternal soul, and it is one of the primary reasons I felt inspired of God to write this book.

Hell-Fire and Damnation

It is intriguing to me that so many of those who classify themselves as atheists or agnostics (and a shocking number of professing Christians, too) like to scorn the biblical teaching and preaching about Hell and divine judgment. They point out how unjust or unloving they think it would be for God to create such a place as Hell, let alone to condemn anyone to spend eternity there. In response to their misunderstanding, let me clarify that, although God did indeed create a place of punishment called Hell, He doesn't condemn or send *any human being* there without first offering them the opportunity to escape it—*multiple times*. Therefore, by providing a means of escape from Hell and offering it to every person who ever lives, it is each individual's own choice to go to Hell when he or she rejects God's Plan of Salvation.

It's a little like being in a high-rise apartment building with a fire escape at the end of the building. Before a fire, the manager can post signs all around the building pointing in the direction of the fire escape and warning not to take the stairs or elevator during a fire. He can warn people in fire safety classes, in tenant newsletters, and in one-on-one conversations to follow these instructions. In the actual event of a fire, the building manager can sound the alarm and maybe even rush door-to-door alerting people to the danger of the fire and warning them that the only way of escape is through the fire escape at the end of the building, but it's up to the residents to accept the manager's word and follow his instructions to exit via the fire escape. While this analogy is not a perfect example, I hope it makes the point, nonetheless. God can send us all kinds of warnings right up until the time we die and are engulfed by the fire of Hell, but it's entirely up to us whether we choose to believe His Word and heed His warnings.

According to Jesus, the reason God created Hell in the first place was as a punishment for "the devil and his angels" (Matthew 25:41). Since God does not tell us *why* it was necessary to create such a place of punishment, we can only speculate. Moreover, we must be very careful in our speculations, because such musings can lead us astray into falsehood. Thus, anything which we cannot validate by the written Word of God–*The Holy Bible*– is suspect and must not be taught as truth.

So, just how bad *is* Hell anyway? I mean, would it be so bad to have to spend eternity there after all? Will Hell be filled with partiers celebrating their permanent independence from Almighty God? Once again, according to Jesus' descriptions, Hell is a truly horrible place, the *most* horrible place, in fact, in all of God's creation. Perhaps that's why Jesus spoke more about Hell than He did about Heaven during His earthly ministry. He doesn't want *anyone* to go there (see 2 Peter 3:9)! Hell is a place of everlasting torment by fire for many (Luke 16:22-24) and a place of "outer darkness" for others (Matthew 8:12; 22:13; and 25:30), reinforcing again the idea of levels of punishment there. It is a place of corruption that never ceases, where even the worms are immortal (Mark 9:43-48; Isaiah 66:24). You see, *everyone* is going to live forever; it's just a question of *where* we will spend eternity.

Hell is a place of terrible anguish and suffering–both emotionally and bodily–that produces weeping, wailing, and gritting of teeth (Matthew 8:12; 13:42; 13:50; 22:13; 24:51; 25:30; and Luke 13:28). In short, it is a place completely absent and devoid of any of God's mercy, grace, compassion, love, or protection. For those who wish to have nothing to do with God, He will have nothing to do with them–forever and ever. It is indeed the saddest fact about the most awful place of all time. In fact, perhaps the most awful fact of all about Hell is the absolute hopelessness of ever escaping.

In my roles as both a pastor and a military chaplain, I've talked with some deeply misguided people over the years who think that they can negotiate a different outcome with God once they stand before Him for judgment. My friend, this could not be further from the truth! As Hebrews 9:27 states, ". . . it is appointed for men to die once, but after this the judgment. . . ." Our decision is final, and our fate is sealed once we depart this life. Only a resurrection from death back to mortal life will afford one a second chance. There will be no opportunity for renegotiation of our fate when we stand before His judgment seat. Even as Jesus stood silent before His accusers, despite being innocent, we will stand silent before Him at our judgment *because of our guilt*. Therefore, whether we stand before Him as believers at the Bema Seat (as referenced in Romans 14:10 and 2 Corinthians 5:10) or whether we stand before Him at the Great White Throne for judgment (Revelation 20:11-15), there will be nothing we can say to defend ourselves. We will simply receive our reward—whether good or bad—according as He deems fitting. Let me hasten to add here, however, that the Bema Seat Judgment for believers is not to determine whether we get to enter Heaven, but rather it is to determine what manner of rewards we will receive for the works we did while we lived on earth (see 1 Corinthians 3:10-15), because the Bema Seat Judgment takes place *in Heaven*, while the Great White Throne Judgment takes place beside (or possibly above) the Lake of Fire after the end of Jesus' millennial reign (see Revelation 20:11-15).

Since God is supremely righteous, I believe it was necessary for Him to create Hell to separate those who choose to live in any way other than according to His standard of divine righteousness, as well as those who, despite living a somewhat good and moral life, choose not to accept His covenant for salvation. Moreover, when God created Hell, He knew full well that His most beloved creation—humanity, the only one created in His own image, according to Genesis 1:26—would likewise fall prey to Satan's deception, and that the majority of humankind would end up in this terrible place (see Matthew 7:13-14). Nevertheless, I believe further that He decided it was worth the cost to save even a fraction of human beings for eternal, loving fellowship with Him (compare Hebrews 12:1-2). After all, God would give every human being the power to make his or her own decision about whether to believe God's Word and whether to live with Him in eternal loving fellowship and righteousness. It is this tremendous power of choice which makes every one of us totally responsible for where we spend eternity. Not only did God grant us the ability to choose our eternal destiny, but He also paid the price for the sins of all humankind, so that He could righteously justify each one of us simply for believing His Word and asking for His salvation.

What About Those Who Haven't Heard God's Word?

You may ask, "But what about those people who live in remote places far from modern civilization? How can they choose to believe God's Word when they don't even have a copy of it in their own native language?" Once again, God has covered all the bases. According to the Apostle Paul,

> For the wrath of God is revealed from heaven against all ungodliness and unrighteousness of men, who suppress the truth in unrighteousness, because **what may be known of God is manifest in them, for God has shown *it* to them. For since the creation of the world His invisible *attributes* are clearly seen, being understood by the things that are made, *even* His eternal power and Godhead, so that they are without excuse, because, although they knew God, they did not glorify *Him* as God, nor were thankful, but became futile in their thoughts, and their foolish hearts were darkened** (Romans 1:18-21; emphasis added).

Even someone living in the remotest parts of the earth can see the "invisible *attributes*" of God in his or her own body and in God's beautiful creation and wonder how it came into being. It is at that moment in time that the Holy Spirit of God speaks to that questing human heart and takes credit for the glorious works of creation. *No one* can examine the natural wonders of creation without asking how it came into being, and every time such a person asks the question, God always speaks up and invites him or her to believe and trust in Him. Even without a copy of *The Holy Bible* translated into their native language for them to read and study, God will initiate His everlasting covenant with them and write their name in His Book of Life if they will only believe. Furthermore, every time someone's faulty world view (such as belief in the theory of evolution) is challenged by the Word of God, the Spirit of God speaks to their heart and invites them to believe His truth. All too often, however, they simply dismiss the voice of God as a preposterous thought in support of a belief system they have already rejected. God will judge everyone based on the degree of revelation they have received. The more revelation one has, the lesser the excuse he or she will have in missing or rejecting the truth about God. As Jesus said:

> And that servant who knew his master's will, and did not prepare *himself* or do according to his will, shall be beaten with many *stripes*. But he who did not know, yet committed things deserving of stripes, shall be beaten with few. **For everyone to whom much is given, from him much will be required; and to whom much has been committed, of him they will ask the more** (Luke 12:47-48; emphasis added).

This implies there will be levels of punishment in Hell, even as there will be levels of reward in the Kingdom of God. For a few examples of the latter, read Matthew 25:14-30, Romans 14:10 and 2 Corinthians 5:10.

Taking God at His Word

Because it is impossible for God to lie (see Titus 1:2 and Hebrews 6:18), it is also impossible for God to let anyone get by with rejecting the truth of His Word (see Hebrews 11:6 and 1 John 5:10). In fact, it was doubting the truthfulness of God's Word that prompted Adam and Eve to violate God's commandment in the Garden of Eden in the first place (see Genesis 3:1-6). Believing and accepting God's Word as absolute truth, then, has been the key to God's Plan of Salvation ever since. As the Apostle Paul pointed out,

"For what does the Scripture say? 'ABRAHAM BELIEVED GOD, AND IT WAS ACCOUNTED TO HIM FOR RIGHTEOUSNESS'" (Romans 4:3 as quoted from Genesis 15:6). **Thus, taking God at His Word has been God's means of salvation from sin and Hell from the very beginning, and it remains so even until now.** Of course, it was still necessary for Jesus to atone for all human sin with His sinless blood and rise from the dead, too (compare Romans 10:8-10 & 1 Corinthians 15:17).

The judgment of God and punishment for our sins may be rightfully averted, if only we will believe His Word–the Bible–and accept and obey its teachings as absolute truth. On the other hand, if we try to filter His Word as only partially true, we open ourselves up to error and endanger our very souls. After all, if you can't believe God is truthful in saying He created the universe in six 24-hour days, how can you trust Him to be truthful in promising to save your soul from Hell? And if you can't believe that God has the power to do supernatural feats, such as preserving Jonah in the belly of a great fish for three days and nights or parting the Red Sea or parting the Jordan River or causing a virgin girl to conceive the Messiah or to raise that Messiah from death, how can you believe He can or will save your soul from Hell?

Hell is an awful place to spend eternity with no hope of ever being released! When the Word of God so clearly states that all one must do to escape this terrible place is to believe God's Word and accept His Plan of Salvation by trusting in Jesus and

His saving work, why on earth would you take such a risk with your everlasting soul?

Comparatively speaking, I seriously doubt that you would liquidate everything you own into cash, take it to the nearest roulette table, plop it down and wage the entire bundle of bills on one spin of the wheel (unless, of course, you are truly bound up with an addiction to gambling). Yet, by waiting even one more second without a covenant with God you could easily slip into eternity and spend that eternity in an awful place called Hell. Not a one of us has a guarantee of even our next breath. How much more valuable is your soul than all the wealth you can amass! In fact, Jesus said it this way:

> For what profit is it to a man if he gains the whole world, and loses his own soul? Or **what will a man give in exchange for his soul?** (Matthew 16:26; emphasis added).

Multiple writers and speakers from history have said (in one form or another) that there are only two certainties in life: death and taxes. Furthermore, according to the Scripture, ". . .it is appointed for men to die once, but after this the judgment. . ." (Hebrews 9:27). However, for those who are counted worthy to be included in the Rapture, not even death is certain! (Compare Luke 21:36; John 11:25-26; 1 Corinthians 15:51-52; 1 Thessalonians 4:13-17; and Revelation 3:10.)

The ultimate judgment of God will take place after we die. Nevertheless, for the believer (that is, the one who believes God's Word and strives to live by it) the judgment for sin has already been settled by Jesus. Jesus' death on the cross atoned for and paid for *all* human sin (though it applies only to those who believe and accept this as true) and His resurrection from the dead demonstrates His power not only over death but over sin and its everlasting punishment, too. The judgment of God is therefore reserved for those *without* an everlasting covenant with Him.

Although Jesus spoke more about Hell than He did about Heaven (presumably, because He wanted everyone to avoid the place), it is Heaven we all want to dwell in forever. Deeply committed Christians dream of it almost every day. We sing of it in our hymns and contemporary songs; we listen to sermons and Bible lessons about it; and we talk about it with our fellow believers. However, to receive the blessed benefit of everlasting love, joy, and peace, we must be willing to believe God's Word, accept His Plan of Salvation (as detailed in His Word) and engage in His everlasting covenant with Him. I'll talk more about this hope of everlasting life in the next chapter. It's the very bedrock upon which our hope is based. It is also the earnest and fervent desire of God's heart to have us there with Him in His Kingdom forever (see Luke 13:32).

CHAPTER TEN: EVERLASTING LIFE

Perhaps what happens after death has been one of humanity's greatest concerns since the first funeral in human history. According to the Bible, Adam and Eve, the ones who introduced mortality into human existence, were not the first to experience this transition from life on this plane of existence to life on the next plane of existence. Their son, Cain, killed their son, Abel (Genesis 4:8), which may have stirred up in their hearts all sorts of uncertainties. Where did Abel go after he died, and what would become of Cain because of his terrible act? When would their turn to die come, and what would it be like to die?

God had warned Adam (who must have certainly conveyed this warning to Eve after she was created later that same day) that they would surely die if they ate the forbidden fruit (Genesis 2:16-17), yet they had continued to live in their physical bodies. Was God referring to a spiritual death (as most theologians teach) or was He referring to their bodily death, which would eventually take place in the process of time? If Adam and Eve died spiritually on the day they ate the forbidden fruit, when were they then reborn, since Jesus said that no one may "see the kingdom of God" without first being reborn (John 3:3-8)? Finally, did Adam and Eve have any idea of when they would eventually die? While answering any or all these questions may not give us the insight into Adam and Eve's minds that we desire, maybe the exercise will at least help us imagine what they thought about life after death and what they were expecting to happen after they died.

Actually, the Bible does not give us any obvious insight into what Adam and Eve thought about Paradise or life after death, but having walked with God for at least a day or so into the first week after creation before they sinned, they almost certainly had some idea that life after death would mean uninterrupted fellowship with God ever after. This appears to me to be the one aspect of life after death that nominal believers in God overlook, since only truly committed believers in Jesus Christ ever mention it as the primary reason for having an everlasting life after the end of our present existence on earth.

Everyone–nominal and committed believers alike–refers to Heaven as the peaceful rest of our soul where we will dwell in comfort and safety forever and ever, but if nominal believers think to mention the presence of God or Jesus with them as part of the experience, it is usually an apparent afterthought. Yet, it is this fellowship with God that makes our life after death possible in the first place. Were it not for God's presence, there would be no peace or rest or safety and security to enjoy. In short, there would be no experience of what we believe Heaven to be at all.

What Is Heaven?

The very word *Heaven* refers to the location of God's dwelling (see Psalm 123:1) and the Scriptures also tell us, "You [God] will show me the path of life; In Your presence is fullness of joy; At Your right hand are pleasures forevermore" (Psalm 16:11). Indeed, the very word *Heaven* has come to be a metaphor for everything wonderfully pleasant that we feebleminded human beings can imagine. Without God, however, there *is no* Heaven. It is this metaphorical idea of everything pleasant that makes the notion of everlasting life *truly Heaven*. Therefore, I chose to call this chapter "Everlasting Life" rather than "Heaven"–because having everlasting life is what we all mean when we say we want to go to Heaven. We mean that we want to live forever in a blissful place called Heaven.

So, how can you know whether you are a nominal believer in God or a truly committed believer in God through His Son Jesus Christ? It's as easy as what you expect Heaven to be like when (or if) you get there. For instance, is the joy of being in Heaven all about you and those you care about, or is it about *God* and those *He* cares about? You see, your understanding of your relationship with God in Heaven is what sorts out whether you are a nominal believer in God or a truly committed believer in God. Let me say that if your relationship with God through His Son

Jesus Christ is not the primary focus of your desire for being in Heaven, then you are a nominal believer in God, and until your heart changes in this regard, you will remain a nominal believer. Unfortunately, a nominal believer is somewhat less likely to reach Heaven, because of this skewed view of the whole purpose of Heaven. Heaven is God's reward to those who desire an eternal, intimate relationship with *Him*. As genuinely wonderful as it is going to be to live in Heaven forever, without God as our primary focus and reason for being there, it's akin to desiring to be married to a wealthy person so we can enjoy his or her wealth without ever having to interact with him or her as our spouse! What kind of marriage would *that* be? If you put yourself in the place of the wealthy person, how loved by your spouse would you feel if you learned that he or she had married you strictly to enjoy your wealth and blessings but not your presence? Would you wish to remain married to this person? Would you desire to spend any time with this person knowing he or she did not feel toward you the same love you felt toward him or her?

Imagine now that God is in the place of the wealthy spouse, and we are in the place of this self-centered, parasitical spouse. Believe it or not, God knows that we do not love Him to the same reciprocal degree as He loves us, yet He still desires to have us with Him in His Heaven forever. Nevertheless, what kind of relationship can we expect to have with God if we desire to enjoy all the benefits of His Heaven without desiring to enjoy the pleasure of His presence? Surely, even if we do not love God as strongly as He loves us, can we not desire to grow in our love for Him, nonetheless?

If you are a nominal believer in God with more of an eye toward what you can gain from the joy of Heaven than with how you can love God in return for all He has done for you, then how do you differ from the self-centered, parasitical spouse described above? Despite the fact that God knows our level of love for Him does not equal His love for us, do you think He wants us ever to grow to love Him in return or to continue forever in a mostly one-sided living arrangement with Him? If God does not expect us to ever love Him in return, why did Jesus point out the first of what He called the Two Greatest Commandments, "You shall love the LORD your God with all your heart, with all your soul, and with all your strength" (Matthew 22:37; Mark 12:30; and Luke 10:27; compare with Deuteronomy 6:5)? What does *all* mean in these verses? It means *all*, of course! No exceptions; no omissions!

That doesn't sound to me like some weak-willed kind of love that God expects to receive from us. It doesn't sound to me as though God is willing to accept a relationship from us that puts anything or anyone else but Him as first in our hearts and lives, and that includes putting the joys of everlasting life in Heaven above our joy of being with Him. In fact, Jesus went so far as to say,

"If anyone comes to Me and does not hate his father and mother, wife and children, brothers and sisters, yes, and his own life also, he cannot be My disciple" (Luke 14:26).

Does this mean we must despise members of our own family to be a disciple of Jesus Christ? No, it means that when we are confronted with a choice between loving God foremost and loving even our closest relative or our own life foremost, we must choose to love God foremost, and then trust Him to provide for us and those we love. I think this also falls in line with the first of the Ten Commandments: "You shall have no other gods before Me" (Exodus 20:3). "Before" in this instance means "ahead of" or "in front of" God.

If we stop to consider how wonderful it is to feel truly loved by someone else, do you think God desires to experience our love for Him, just as He wants us to experience His love for us? If you truly wish to live in Heaven forever, then consider just a little of what Heaven is going to be like when we finally get there and how we can deepen our love for this truly wonderful God who wants to share it with us.

Where Is Heaven?

Since we have already ascertained that Heaven is the place of God's dwelling, perhaps its location could be better defined as *wherever God is*. According to John's description in Revelation 21:1-7,

> Now I saw a new heaven and a new earth, for the first heaven and the first earth had passed away. Also there was no more sea. **Then I, John, saw the holy city, New**

Jerusalem, coming down out of heaven from God, prepared as a bride adorned for her husband. And I heard a loud voice from heaven saying, "Behold, the tabernacle of God is with men, and He will dwell with them, and they shall be His people. God Himself will be with them and be their God. And God will wipe away every tear from their eyes; there shall be no more death, nor sorrow, nor crying. There shall be no more pain, for the former things have passed away." Then He who sat on the throne said, "Behold, I make all things new." And He said to me, "Write, for these words are true and faithful." And He said to me, "It is done! I am the Alpha and the Omega, the Beginning and the End. I will give of the fountain of the water of life freely to him who thirsts. **He who overcomes shall inherit all things, and I will be his God and he shall be My son**" (emphasis added).

It appears to me that Heaven comes down to earth in this description, because someone shouts, "Behold, the tabernacle of God is with men, and He will dwell with them, and they shall be His people" (Revelation 21:3). Therefore, since "the tabernacle [or dwelling] of God is with men," Heaven will be *among* us. We will not dwell on some fluffy cloud strumming a harp for eternity, but we will dwell in a New Jerusalem on a New Earth with a New Heaven all around us.

When we read the description of the New Jerusalem, we learn that it is an enormous, enclosed city with no windows, lit throughout entirely by the glory of Jesus, the Lamb of God (Revelation 21:23 & 22:5). The city is measured thusly:

> The city is laid out as a square, and its length is as great as the width; and he measured the city with the rod, fifteen

hundred miles; its length and width and height are equal
(Revelation 21:16 NASB).

Can you imagine living in a city that is spread out 1500 miles in nearly every direction–north, south, east, west, and UP? It boggles my brain! I like to call this *one ginormous apartment complex*, since Jesus said, "In My Father's house are many dwelling places; if it were not so, I would have told you; for I go to prepare a place for you" (John 14:2 NASB). Other translations use the word "rooms" in place of "dwelling places," though both are accurate in their depictions. The King James and New King James translations use the word "mansions" for "rooms" or "dwelling places," but while this word depicts the luxurious aspect of our residence in the New Jerusalem, it seems to detract from the communal aspect, since a mansion tends to imply a stand-alone dwelling that is separate and isolated from every other, though it has many rooms of its own where multiple people may dwell. I believe we will have our own space that will be luxurious in every respect, but it will be contained within this single complex that is the New Jerusalem.

Whichever way it is laid out, this is just one of myriads of details designed to overwhelm us with God's love, joy, and grandeur, for besides being 1500 miles square and high, the New Jerusalem will also be built with walls of jasper and the purest of gold, resting upon twelve foundations adorned with twelve different precious stones. The city will also have twelve gates made of one enormous pearl for each gate (three gates on each of the four sides of the city) and a street of the purest gold. This entire description is contained in Revelation 21:18-20.

Flowing from the throne of God within the city will be a pure river of life, clear as crystal (Revelation 22:1). Planted in the middle of the street and on either side of the river of life will be the Tree of Life bearing twelve fruits, a different fruit for each of twelve months (Revelation 22:2). Whoever said time would be no more in Heaven hasn't considered this statement, for how can you live a timeless existence and yet measure twelve different months of fruit production on the Tree of Life alone? Since we measure years by twelve different months now, it appears we will continue to measure months and years for all eternity. One question I have, however, is how long each of these months and years will be. Given that we will be living on a New Earth under a New Heaven, it is entirely possible that God could lengthen the months and years in this New World, but since He hasn't seen fit to reveal that bit of information to us yet, we will just have to wait to see.

I'm sure there's much more to the New Jerusalem and the New Heaven and New Earth that God has not described for us in these passages of Scripture (Revelation chapters 21 and 22), so we will simply have to wait to learn what else He has in store for us when we get there. Of course, getting there requires that we obey His explicit instructions. Failing to heed God's warnings and obey His commands as outlined for us in *The Holy Bible* will effectively disqualify us from receiving this glorious reward, for to ignore God's Word is to ignore and reject God.

Abundant Life

So, to summarize this chapter about everlasting life, Heaven, and what they both mean, let me refer to Jesus' words to His disciples, where He said, ". . . I have come that they may have life, and that they may have it more abundantly" (John 10:10). What is *abundant life*?

To answer that, we must first define the word *abundant*. Webster's Online Dictionary defines it as, "marked by great plenty (as of resources)."[44] I would define *abundant,* then, as having more than enough for what is needed. In other words, abundant life is having more than enough life for living. So, how can we have more than enough life for living? The only way to have that is to have *everlasting life*. As the final verse of the grand old hymn "Amazing Grace" relates: "When we've been there ten thousand years, bright shining as the sun, we've no less days to sing God's praise than when we first begun."[45] Let that sink in for a minute and think about it. Therefore, I think Jesus was referring to eternal life when He spoke the words quoted above in John 10:10.

Part of what makes Heaven so wonderful and attractive is the everlasting life we get to live in absolute contentment. Life filled with pure love, luxury, and unending longevity without physical or mental decline is probably the best description of Heaven that we can possibly imagine or verbalize. In fact, without the everlasting life aspect, none of the other aspects would even be meaningful, because none of the other aspects could be fully enjoyed without everlasting life. Moreover, if life in Heaven was not everlasting, then–except for the aspects of peace and safety and freedom from evil and the Evil One–it would scarcely differ at all from the life we are living right now. How wonderful would life in Heaven be if it would eventually come to another end, just as the life we currently live will one day end? How could we fully enjoy our life in Heaven if we knew it would end again at some point?

Truly, it is the everlasting aspect of life in Heaven that makes it so wonderful and desirable, and we really need to understand that getting into God's Heaven is not something *any* of us is automatically entitled to. It is a glorious reward for believing what God has promised in His Holy Word—the Bible—and for living our life in *this* world as much in accordance with His Word as we possibly can. Indeed, failure to *read* God's Word will ultimately result in our failure to *heed* God's Word, because His Word is where we learn God's requirements for living in *this* world, so that we may be permitted to live forever with Him in the *next* world—Heaven.

So, how can we *know* that we'll get to live forever in this glorious Kingdom of God? I'll cover that in the next chapter.

CHAPTER ELEVEN: SO, HOW CAN I *KNOW* I'M SAVED?

First, I may need to explain what the term "saved" means before I can answer the question posed by this chapter's title. From a biblical standpoint, the word *saved* means rescued by God from the condemnation to Hell that is an automatic result of sin. Since every human being is born with a sin nature and begins committing sins from early childhood, we all grow up as sinners condemned for our sins, which we commit as a result of our sin nature. This very condition automatically disqualifies us from Heaven until we *personally* choose to accept God's Plan of Salvation. Because this Plan of Salvation is not something God was *obligated* to make available to us, we call it an act of God's grace. So then, whoever accepts God's gracious Plan of Salvation is therefore said to be saved by the grace of God.

As for infants, young children and mentally impaired adults who do not have the capacity to understand their sin state and need for pardon, we Christians believe God's grace covers their sins and pardons their souls in the event of their death, based upon Jesus' work of atonement. We base this belief primarily upon the words of Jesus that we are to "receive the kingdom of God as a little child" (Mark 10:15 and Luke 18:17)–referring to their simple faith in whatever anyone tells them–and that "their angels always see the face of My Father who is in heaven" (Matthew 18:10). Jesus also scolded His disciples for shunning the children who were brought to Him for blessing:

> Then they brought little children to Him, that He might touch them; but the disciples rebuked those who brought them. But when Jesus saw it, He was greatly displeased and said to them, **"Let the little children come to Me, and do not forbid them; for of such is the kingdom of God. Assuredly, I say to you, whoever does not receive the kingdom of God as a little child will by no means enter it"** (Mark 10:13-15; emphasis added).

Furthermore, we refer to King David's statement at the death of his newborn son, which he fathered in adultery with Bathsheba, Uriah's wife (see 2 Samuel 12:23). Since we know David expected to "dwell in the house of the LORD Forever" (Psalm 23:6), we learn that David had an assurance from God that he would be reunited with this infant son again after his own death.

Since everyone wants to go to Heaven, and since no one is automatically entitled to live there, the next most important question for *any* of us to resolve is: How can I gain access to this magnificent place to live there forever, and how can I *know for sure* I'm going there? In biblical terminology, this is called "being saved," so let's rephrase the question in biblical terms: How can I *know* I'm saved?

Perhaps you are still wincing over the statement in the previous paragraph (restated from the end of the previous chapter) that no one is automatically entitled to live in Heaven after they die. This is indeed a disturbing thought to consider for most people, but is it true? I mean, *who says* no one is automatically entitled to go to Heaven when they die? Well, *God* says this in *The Holy Bible*, and *The Holy Bible* claims to be God's own words communicated with those of us living in this world.

Can We Really Trust the Bible?

Perhaps one of the biggest hurdles of thought for many people to overcome is whether the Bible *really is* God's inspired word of truth for the world. If we can believe anything at all from the Bible, why can't we believe *all* that is in the Bible? How can only parts of it be inspired by God, while other parts are false? Does it make sense that God would inspire only portions of the Bible and leave us floundering in ignorance about which parts He inspired and which parts He didn't inspire?

It simply requires a small step of faith to believe that God inspired the entirety of the Bible's contents. Not only that, but we can also trust that God shepherded the canonization process of the Bible, too. In other words, He made certain that only those books that He truly inspired were included within the contents of the Bible. Consider this: if God could inspire approximately 40 men (possibly more, since the authorship of some books is unclear) to compose 66 books over a period of about 1500 years, could He also guide those who determined which books to include in the Bible? Furthermore, if God could create the universe, could He also control the composition and compilation of the Bible? If we can believe God created everything and that He inspired the writing of the Scriptures, why can't we believe that He controlled the compilation and canonization of the Bible?

By rejecting outright that the Bible is God's wholly inspired Word of truth, you dismiss God's communication to you and retain your automatic disqualification from Heaven with that one ill-fated decision. For if you can't accept the Bible as God's True Word (when it plainly says that it *is* God's inspired Word—see 2 Timothy 3:16; 2 Peter 1:20-21; & 2 Peter 3:14-16), how then can you accept the God who has asserted that He is the ultimate author of the Bible, while rejecting His Word to you? Moreover, how would we know anything at all about God without the Bible's descriptions to go by? Are you aware that without the Bible we would not know that such a place as Heaven or Hell exists or that God is a God of love and righteousness or that a very evil problem called sin threatens to separate us from God forever if we do not accept God's Plan of Salvation to escape it? The only reason we know anything about either of these concepts, such as sin and righteousness, Heaven and Hell, and salvation from sin and Hell, is because the Bible has explained them to us.

So, without the Bible, we would have no idea at all what it means to be saved or *how* to be saved from God's judgment for our sins. Perhaps it is because we find some of these concepts difficult to accept (such as eternal damnation for a sin nature we were born with) that we naturally want to question their veracity and validity by questioning the validity of whether the Bible is God's inspired Word. We deceive ourselves if we think we can discredit the Bible as God's Word so that we don't have to believe it or accept it or live by it, and that we can therefore ignore it ever after. By discrediting and rejecting the Bible as God's inspired Word, we also reject the God of the Bible as being the One True God, and it just so happens that He is the same God who wants to share eternity with us in Heaven—*if* we will believe His Word and accept it as truth.

Unfortunately, some people try to pick and choose what they believe is inspired by God and what is not. Of course, this causes a major problem for how to rightly discern which parts of the Bible are truly inspired by God and which parts are not. Naturally, the parts which give us the most displeasure and discomfort rise to the top of the list of those parts of the Bible which we may deem to be unbelievable. Again, if we can't believe *all* the Bible, how can we believe *any* of it, since the Bible claims divine inspiration for its *entire* contents?

If, however, we set our displeasure and discomfort aside and accept those unpleasant parts of the Bible (such as a literal Hell as a punishment for our sins), then we can heed the warnings contained in the Bible about the need for a Savior and accept what the Bible has to tell us about who this Savior is and what we must do in order to claim Him as our Savior and receive the salvation which He alone can provide. Once we arrive at this conclusion and make this decision about accepting God's Plan of Salvation, we can believe that we will be permitted into God's Heaven to live with Him forever. Now, I'd like to use the remainder of this chapter to explain what this Plan of Salvation is and how to enter it and know for certain that we are *truly saved.*

"What Must I Do To Be Saved?"

This is the question posed by the Philippian jailer to the Apostles Paul and Silas in Acts 16:30. Essentially, we can take Paul and Silas' response to the Philippian jailer's question as God's pronouncement for what *any* of us must do in order to be saved: "So they said, 'Believe on the Lord Jesus Christ, and you will be saved, you and your household'" (Acts 16:31). Notice Paul and Silas did not rattle off a long list of things for the jailer to do to be saved, such as being circumcised, obeying the Law of Moses, or even receiving water baptism. It was the simple faith in Jesus as His Lord and Savior that accomplished the work of salvation. As Paul wrote in his letter to the Ephesians,

> **For by grace you have been saved through faith, and that not of yourselves; it is the gift of God, not of works, lest anyone should boast.** For we are His workmanship, created in Christ Jesus for good works, which God prepared beforehand that we should walk in them (Ephesians 2:8-10; emphasis added).

From these few verses, we learn that we are saved *by* God's grace *through* placing our faith in Jesus Christ, but *we do good works afterward* as a proof of our relationship with Jesus ever after. So,

Paul is not saying that good works are unimportant, but rather he is saying that although they do not play a role in our salvation, they *do* form the basis upon which we will be rewarded in the Kingdom of God once we arrive there. I like to say it this way: we do not do good works *in order to be saved*; we do good works *because we are saved.*

A Matter of Faith

Friends, this is *not* a complex or complicated matter. It's simply *a matter of faith.* Since the Bible tells us about itself that it is the God-breathed Word of God (2 Timothy 3:16 and 2 Peter 1:21), either you believe and accept what the *entire* Bible says, or you don't. That's all there is to it. It truly is an all-or-nothing proposition.

Of course, there's where the rub comes in for those who simply won't accept the truth, the whole truth, and nothing but the truth as God has so clearly stated it. They will either reject the Bible's authenticity as being God's divinely inspired Word, or they will choose to restate His Word in such a way as to obfuscate its originally clear truth, or they will choose a cleverly devised interpretation that either waters down the meaning or alters it entirely. These are all very dangerous approaches indeed!

To modify God's Word to suit your own preferences is to invite divine judgment (compare Revelation 22:18-19). Not only that, but the Apostle James warns us that teachers of the Word will be judged with greater severity (James 3:1) than rank and file believers. To reject the clearly revealed truth in God's Word is to reject God, and to disbelieve God's Word is synonymous with calling God a liar (1 John 5:10 and Romans 3:4b). This is true whether we're talking about accepting the stories of biblical creation, the global flood, or Jonah being swallowed by a great fish as literally true, or whether we're talking about accepting Jesus Christ as the virgin-born Son of God and Savior of the world. The same Holy Spirit of God inspired the recording of *all* these events. So, if you can muster the faith to accept *some* of the Bible as God's inspired Word, *how can you **not** believe **everything** that is in the Bible?* As the bumper sticker adage that was popular several decades ago states, "God said it. I believe it. That settles it."

One way to get a true perspective on each of these events is to compare what Jesus had to say about them. For instance, Jesus referred to the creation, the Flood, and Jonah in the belly of the great fish as if these were all true stories (Mark 10:6; 13:19; Matthew 24:37-39 & 12:40). Now, shall we doubt Jesus' understanding of either of these Scriptures? Can we trust that He knew what He should and should not believe? Would He advocate and present something as truth that wasn't true?

Perhaps foremost among those who have tinkered with the truth of the Scriptures are those cultic groups who go door-to-door spreading their perversions of God's Word, which they claim are either a more accurate translation or are a superseding addition to the Bible. Nevertheless, cultic groups are not the only ones who actively engage in twisting the truth of the Scriptures. Still, other groups that are even accepted and included as bona fide Christian denominations either misinterpret certain tenets of Scripture, such as the doctrine of pre-destination, or they completely ignore more than half the body of Scripture, better known as the Old Testament, claiming it no longer applies to us today. If that is true, what did the Apostle Paul mean when he wrote,

> For whatever things were written before [he means in the Old Testament Scriptures, because those were the only Scriptures they had at that time] were written for our learning, that we through the patience and comfort of the Scriptures might have hope (Romans 15:4).

Furthermore, what did he mean when he stated,

> Now all these things happened to them as examples, and they were written [again, he means in the Old Testament Scriptures] for our admonition, upon whom the ends of the ages have come (1 Corinthians 10:11).

Why did Paul use the Old Testament Scriptures to make his theological points about God's Plan of Salvation in his epistles to the Church? Well, primarily, he used them because those were the only truly inspired Scriptures in existence at the time. The *New Testament* Scriptures hadn't been completed and compiled yet. In fact, I wonder whether Paul even realized he was adding to the body of Scripture (which would later be defined as *New Testament* Scriptures) by writing the letters he wrote to all the churches.

However, it appears that the Apostle Peter, at least, believed that Paul's writings were divinely inspired Scriptures, because he wrote,

> Nevertheless we, according to His promise, look for new heavens and a new earth in which righteousness dwells. Therefore, beloved, looking forward to these things, be diligent to be found by Him in peace, without spot and blameless; and consider that the longsuffering of our Lord is salvation—**as also our beloved brother Paul, according to the wisdom given to him, has written to you, as also in all his epistles, speaking in them of these things, in which are some things hard to understand, which untaught and unstable people twist to their own destruction, as they do also the rest of the Scriptures** (2 Peter 3:13-16; emphasis added).

That last phrase, "the rest of the Scriptures," demonstrates that Peter, under the same divine inspiration of the same Holy Spirit, included Paul's letters with the *rest of the holy Scriptures,* what we now call the Old Testament Scriptures. It also highlights what Peter called, again by divine inspiration, "untaught and unstable people [who] twist [the Scriptures] to their own destruction." That's quite a statement indeed! It proves to us that we must take great care when interpreting what the Bible has to say, because it's not just another book that we can take or leave when we agree or disagree with its contents. As the Apostle James warns us,

> "My brethren, let not many of you become teachers [he means of the Word of God, in particular], knowing that we shall receive a stricter judgment" (James 3:1).

This includes, I believe, film and stage productions in which so-called literary or dramatic license is taken with the Scriptural account either to omit offensive portions, such as politically incorrect positions, or to add in dialogue that simply isn't present in the original to (supposedly) have more dramatic effect. Such alterations are misleading at the least and misinforming at the worst. It's bad enough when done to other books; it simply should *never* be done to the Bible.

The Apostle Peter also tells us:

> . . . knowing this first, that **no prophecy of Scripture is of any private interpretation,** for prophecy never came by the will of man, but holy men of God spoke as they were moved by the Holy Spirit (2 Peter 1:20-21; emphasis added).

Don't let the word "prophecy" in this passage confuse you, because it includes much more than foretelling the future alone. The underlying Greek word, *propheteia* (pronounced prof-ay-TIE-ah, Strong's G4394, προφητεία)[46] is defined by W. E. Vine as follows:

> . . .Though much of OT prophecy was purely predictive, see Micah 5:2, e.g., and cf. John 11:51, prophecy is not necessarily, nor even primarily, fore-telling. It is the declaration of that which cannot be known by natural means, Matthew 26:68, it is the forth-telling of the will of God, whether with reference to the past, the present, or the future. . . . [47]

This means that an individual can't just invent his or her own interpretation of a Scriptural account or statement just to be different or to soothe his or her own sensibilities. While some Scriptures can have more than one meaning or application, we must be extremely cautious about reading something more into a text than is present. If an interpretation conflicts with another already biblically stated interpretation, it must be dropped from further consideration as a viable interpretation, because it is simply *impossible* for God to contradict Himself.

One truly wonderful aspect of the Bible is that it frequently interprets itself. For instance, after reading "And Enoch walked with God; and he was not, for God took him" (Genesis 5:24), we are left wondering what happened to him. Did God take his life and bury him in a secret grave, as He did with Moses (Deuteronomy 34:5-6), or did God transport him off the earth and into the heavenly realm, as He did with Elijah (2 Kings 2:11-18)? When we come to the New Testament, however, we learn what really happened.

> By faith Enoch was taken away so that **he did not see death,** 'AND WAS NOT FOUND, BECAUSE GOD HAD TAKEN HIM'; for before he was taken he had this testimony, that he pleased God (Hebrews 11:5; emphasis added).

If we can't accept the Bible as the truly inspired Word of God, how can we know what we should believe or how we can be saved? If the Bible is unreliable as a source of truth, how can we know anything at all about God, since everything we presently know about Him is what is revealed to us in the Bible? For instance, we know that He is a God of love, grace, and mercy because the Bible tells us so. We know that He has gone to extreme lengths to make a way for us to escape the punishment for our sins so we can live with Him forever, because this is what the Bible has told us. We know that to enjoy this eternal relationship with Him we must accept His Plan of Salvation made possible and available through His Son, Jesus Christ. We know that God predestines us for everlasting life with Him through His omniscience because the Bible tells us so (Romans 8:29).

From the very beginning of creation, God is presented in the Bible as a covenant-making and covenant-keeping God. If He says He will do something, He does it. If God should ever fail to keep His Word about *anything whatsoever*, He would no longer be trustworthy, and we would then have a good cause to accuse Him of unfairness and injustice. Since God has never failed to keep His Word, however, not only is He eternally just, but He is ever more worthy of our absolute trust. Entering a covenant with God is as simple and easy as believing God's Word is true, and then accepting and obeying what that Word says to do, namely, to believe in who Jesus is and what He did by dying on the cross and rising from the dead.

So, How Can I *Know* I'm Saved?

Okay, we've come back full circle now to our original question: How can I *know* I'm saved? It's as simple as first knowing *what* we are to believe (which God has outlined very clearly for us in the Bible, and which I've expounded upon throughout this book), and then, after accepting and believing it, *trusting in* (i.e., *depending upon*) that knowledge ever after. In other words, the Bible tells us that we are saved by believing God's Word (the Bible) as the absolute truth, that God came into the world as a human being named Jesus, lived a sinless life, died a savage death on a Roman cross as a substitutionary atoning sacrifice for *all* human sin, and raised Himself up to life again after three days in the tomb. Furthermore, He ascended back into Heaven to prepare a permanent dwelling place for all who accept His saving work on earth and to await the pre-appointed time when He will return to earth to set up His earthly Kingdom and execute judgment on His enemies (i.e., those who choose to reject Him and His offer of salvation as described in the Bible).

My friend, if you can believe and accept each one of these tenants of God's Word and live your life accordingly, then you can have **absolute confidence** that the God who cannot lie will keep His promise to save all who believe His promised Words. In other words, you can *know* you're saved because of *what* you believe and *who* you've placed your confidence and trust in. It's just that simple!

Overcoming Your Doubts

One of Satan's most pernicious strategies is to cause God's people to doubt their salvation because of personal guilt over past sins or even over recent sins committed since becoming a Christian. If he can't prevent people from believing in and accepting the truth of God's Word in the first place, he will attempt to dissuade them from their confidence in God's promise of salvation *after* their commitment to Jesus. In other words, if he can't prevent you from trusting in Jesus to *be* saved, he'll try to prevent you from trusting in Jesus that you *have* been saved. This is specifically why Jesus said,

> My sheep hear My voice, and I know them, and they follow Me. **And I give them eternal life, and they shall never perish; neither shall anyone snatch them out of My hand. My Father, who has given *them* to Me, is greater than all; and no one is able to snatch *them* out of My Father's hand.** I and *My* Father are one (John 10:27-30; emphasis added).

You see, neither Satan nor anyone else can snatch us out of God's omnipotent hand. While it is possible for us to extricate *ourselves* from God's grasp by committing apostasy, this is *not* something we can do inadvertently or in a state of being uninformed. Apostasy is a deliberate and conscious *abandonment* of one's former religious faith. We can't *accidentally* lose our salvation, either by misplacing it or by having it stolen from us. The same is true of committing the infamous unpardonable sin. In both cases, we must necessarily *choose* to reject what we once chose to accept, and just as God honors our choice to accept His offer, He also honors our choice to renounce our former decision. He will not force us to be in His eternal Kingdom if we truly wish not to be there, and this is true whether we reject His offer from the start or whether we accept His offer and then decide later we've made a wrong decision and choose to renounce it. This is what the very word *apostate* means—it is one who has departed from a position of former faith. According to the Apostle Paul, this decision is irreversible for those who "have tasted the heavenly gift, and have become partakers of the Holy Spirit" (Hebrews 6:4-6). Jesus essentially said the same thing when He said, ". . . 'No one, having put his hand to the plow, and looking back, is fit for the kingdom of God'" (Luke 9:62). This further connects with Paul's words in Hebrews 10:38, "Now the just shall live by faith: But if anyone draws back, My soul has no pleasure in him." The Greek word which is translated as "draws back" here is *hupostello* (pronounced *hoop-os-TEL-lo*; Strong's G5288; ὑποστέλλω),[48] and it literally means to withdraw, cower, or shrink back, as in cowardice. For further insight, compare Thayer's more detailed and descriptive definition of this word.[49] Interestingly, "the cowardly" are listed first among those in Revelation 21:8 who will be cast into the Lake of Fire.

So long as we maintain our faith in Jesus, His saving work on the cross on our behalf, and His resurrection from the dead (see 1 Corinthians 15:17 and Romans 10:8-10), we can rest assured that He will keep His promise to save all those who believe in and accept that as the truth (Romans 10:11). It's a matter of faith.

On the other hand, once we begin chipping away at the facts presented to us in the Bible based on some scientific and/or archaeological discoveries that supposedly contradict biblical assertions, then we are drifting into dangerous territory. Since our salvation is based on our faith in God and His

Word, refuting biblical positions and teachings because they defy natural understandings fails to consider the supernatural aspects of the Scripture. God Himself is supernatural, so anything He says or does, whether in the Bible or in our contemporary experience, that opposes natural occurrences ought to be understood as supernatural and unexplainable in any other way. The question quickly becomes one of which god we believe in, if not the God of the Bible. Even atheists have made something or someone their god (e.g., their blind faith in the unprovable theory of evolution), whether they realize it or not. As far as the God of the Bible is concerned, there is no other god besides Him (see Deuteronomy 32:39; Isaiah 45:21-23; and Isaiah 46:8-10). Disbelief of God's Word (the Bible) is synonymous with disbelief of God Himself, for we cannot separate God from His Word. Indeed, the Apostle John has even written that God's Word *is* God (John 1:1). To reject any part of His Word as untrue or untrustworthy is essentially calling God a liar, and the Scripture tells us it is impossible for God to lie (Titus 1:2 and Hebrews 6:18). Moreover, "without faith *it is* impossible to please *Him* [God]" (Hebrews 11:6). Thus, I interpret these biblical accounts as blanket statements and requirements for a right relationship with God. In the end, it is God who will decide whether to save any of those who have rejected the truth of His Word while asking to be pardoned and saved. As the Apostle Paul put it:

> What shall we say then? Is there unrighteousness with God? Certainly not! For He says to Moses, "I WILL HAVE MERCY ON WHOMEVER I WILL HAVE MERCY, AND I WILL HAVE COMPASSION ON WHOMEVER I WILL HAVE COMPASSION." **So then it is not of him who wills, nor of him who runs, but of God who shows mercy"** (Romans 9:14-16; emphasis added).

Ultimately, it is up to God to show grace and mercy unto whomever He wills. I have said many times, both from the pulpit and during conversation, that if God will just allow me into His everlasting Kingdom, I will not dare try to tell Him who to keep out. Even so, I would not want to be in the position of awaiting a decision from God as to whether He will show me mercy and grace *despite* my unbelief when I am already *guaranteed* His grace and pardon (by His Holy Word) when I *believe* His Word *entirely*! What about you? Why would *anyone* want to gamble with his or her soul in such a fashion? As stated in the letter to the Hebrews: "It is a fearful thing to fall into the hands of the living God" (Hebrews 10:31).

Therefore, if the Bible says Jesus was born of a virgin, I believe it. If the Bible says Jonah was swallowed by a great fish and kept there for three days and nights, I believe it. If the Bible says God created the universe in six literal days 6,000 years ago with absolutely no hint of a process called evolution or of billions of years between the creation of the universe and the creation of mankind, I believe it. And there are numerous other examples of supernatural events described in the Bible, many of which I can't fully understand or explain now, yet I accept and believe them *all* as truth, because they are contained in *The Holy Bible*, God's inspired Word. I take them at face value as truth because God has said in the Bible that they are true. I will eagerly await God's revelation of the facts that I don't fully understand now once I am enjoying eternal life with Him in His glorious coming Kingdom. Of course, by then, it may not matter to me anymore.

If you want to *know* you're saved and headed for eternal life in the Heavenly New Jerusalem with Jesus, simply accept and believe as absolute truth everything that the Bible says is true and everything the Bible says is required of us for salvation. Just like Father Abraham, God will count your faith for righteousness unto you (see Genesis 15:6; Romans 4:3-5 & 16-25; and Galatians 3:5-9). It truly is just that simple! I think that's what it means to abide in God's Word, too.

Biblical Proofs of Salvation

If you still feel that you need more proof of your own salvation, try examining yourself using the following Scriptures. First, the Lord Jesus tells us that if we have accepted Him as our personal Savior, we *will* be reborn by the Holy Spirit and saved (John 3:3-18). How can we tell if we've really been reborn? Well, for one thing, our spiritual eyes will be opened, and we will understand spiritual concepts contained in God's Word that we previously could not understand. This does not mean we will understand everything that we read in the Bible after our regeneration, but it does mean that we will understand a great many more things than we could prior to our conversion. For another thing, Jesus tells us that His disciples will be known by their love for one another (John 13:34-35). "One another" here refers to fellow believers in Jesus, not the entire world, though believers in Jesus will also love those in the world who are seeking the One True God and His salvation. The Apostle John tells us that if we have true Christian love in our heart and show it toward our brothers and sisters in Christ, and if we truly accept Jesus as God's Son, then that is a sure sign that we are saved. Specifically, he says:

> In this the children of God and the children of the devil are manifest: **Whoever does not practice right-eousness is not of God, nor *is* he who does not love his brother. . . . Beloved, let us love one another, for love is of God; and everyone who loves is born of God and knows God. He who does not love does not know God, for God is love. . . . By this we know that we abide in Him, and He in us, because He has given us of His Spirit. . . . Whoever confesses that Jesus is the Son of God, God abides in him, and he in God** (1 John 3:10; 4:7-8, 13 & 15; emphasis added).

How can we know that God has given us His Holy Spirit? We will demonstrate both the fruit and the gifts of the Holy Spirit as the Apostle Paul delineates for us in Galatians 5:22-23, Romans 12:6-9, and 1 Corinthians 12:7-11. Despite there being nine items listed in Galatians 5:22-23, note that they are all collectively called "the fruit" (singular) of the Holy Spirit. Therefore, we won't, for instance, demonstrate the joy of the

Spirit without also demonstrating the love and the peace of the Holy Spirit. It's not a pick-and-choose proposition but an all-of-the-above proposition.

Finally, the Apostle Paul tells us that if we verbally confess that Jesus is our Lord and believe in our heart that He resurrected from the dead, then we *will* be saved (Romans 10:9-10). If we are sincere in our confession, we will be regenerated on the spot, and the signs of our regeneration—i.e., love for Christ and His people and the demonstration of both the fruit and the gifts of the Holy Spirit—will follow very soon thereafter. In addition to each of these depictions, we will also desire and strive to do good works as described in the Bible, because, as new creatures in Christ, we have been re-created for good works (2 Corinthians 5:17; Galatians 6:15; and Ephesians 2:10).

All these passages reveal to us various proofs of how we can *know beyond any doubt* that we belong to Christ and are saved for His Eternal Kingdom. Personally, I think the strongest proof is in whether we express the genuine love of Christ, which is the very first item on the list that constitutes the fruit of the Holy Spirit:

> But the fruit of the Spirit is love, joy, peace, longsuffering, kindness, goodness, faithfulness, gentleness, self-control. Against such there is no law (Galatians 5:22-23).

Moreover, the Apostle Paul tells us: "For all the law is fulfilled in one word, even in this: 'YOU SHALL LOVE YOUR NEIGHBOR AS YOURSELF'" (Galatians 5:14).

One who claims to be a Christian and yet does not accept the Bible as the inspired Word of God or who does not believe everything the Bible has said about Jesus (such as His virgin birth, divinity, and resurrection from the dead) or who does not show genuine godly love toward fellow believers, in particular, as well as those who might become believers, is merely deceiving himself or herself. According to the Scriptures, such a one is not a true believer and is therefore not truly saved, because he or she has not been regenerated in his or her heart and soul. The proof of one's true regeneration is in the difference in attitude and behavior and belief system compared to everyone else in the world. In other words, where there has been no conversion (a change in thinking and behaving) there has been no regeneration (rebirth or spiritual birth). It really is just that clear.

If you have asked Jesus to be your personal Savior and if your life exhibits the true love of Christ, then you can relax and trust in the faithfulness of God that you have been saved, and you will spend eternity with Him in Heaven. Well, really, we will live in the New Jerusalem on the New Earth, but because Jesus will be there, it truly will be Heaven on Earth. Remember Jesus' words to us: "Do not fear, little flock, for it is your Father's good pleasure to give you the kingdom" (Luke 12:32).

You see, God is not looking for ways to keep us *out* of His Kingdom, but rather He has done all He can to help us *enter* His Kingdom—all, that is, except make the choice for us. *That* we must do for ourselves.

Although God will not make the choice for us, He has, in fact, given us the answer to the ultimate multiple-choice test of all time. As He said to the people of Israel through Moses,

> I call heaven and earth as witnesses today against you, that I have set before you life and death, blessing and cursing; **therefore choose life, that both you and your descendants may live. . .** (Deuteronomy 30:19; emphasis added).

I don't know about you, but knowing that God desires to have me in His Eternal Kingdom even more than I desire it for myself is one of the greatest reassurances of all. If you have chosen Christ for yourself and accepted all that the Bible has to say about Him, then you can rest assured that you *will* spend eternity with Him, and I will eagerly look forward to meeting you when we all get there. Perhaps we will even take turns fellowshipping at each other's personally designed space in the New Jerusalem! Amen and amen!

CONCLUSION

It's decision time. If you were an unbeliever before reading this book, whether a rabid anti-believer in Christ or simply an ignorant and/or apathetic unbeliever completely oblivious to the eternal danger awaiting your soul, you have a decision to make now regarding whether you will accept the truth of what you've read in the Bible and in this book. Naturally, the decision is yours to make. God Himself will not force you to accept His Plan of Salvation, but He has said no less than three times in the Bible (once in the Old Testament and twice in the New Testament) that one day every knee *will* bow and every tongue *will* agree that He *is* the Lord God (see Isaiah 45:23; Romans 14:11; and Philippians 2:9-11). Presumably, this will take place at the final judgment. Your decision is no less important than that of the nominal believer mentioned below. However, whereas the nominal believer may or may not actually be safe in the Kingdom of Christ, the unbeliever is most definitely *not* safe in the Kingdom, despite what Pope Francis may have said on December 25, 2013, that *all* people, including atheists, who simply strive to live a "good" life can expect to be accepted by God when Judgment Day comes.[50]

Friend, according to the Bible, that is simply not true! Because it is contra-biblical, it will doom your soul to Hell just as quickly as any other false teaching! Hopefully, you have come to understand the truth about salvation from what you've read in and about the Bible throughout this book you're presently reading.

If you were a nominal believer prior to reading this book, it's time now for you to decide whether you wish to continue giving Christ your leftovers of time, money, affection, etc. and still hope to receive His exorbitantly generous blessing of eternal life with Him, or whether you're finally ready to sell out to Jesus and become one of His most ardent followers hereafter and, by so doing, secure the hope in your heart and mind that you will indeed be included in His Kingdom when the time comes. Only you can truly ascertain, after a seriously close examination of your heart and its motives, whether you are a true believer or merely one who gives lip service to Christ while forging ahead with your own plans and agenda to the exclusion of His Plan of Salvation for you. Frighteningly, you are but one step away from an eternity without Christ in a place of everlasting torment called Hell. I sincerely hope you will give *very* serious consideration to your standing with Jesus Christ right now and determine to draw closer to Him by reading from His Word, the Bible, and striving to live by its commands and heed its warnings from now on.

If you were already a committed believer when you began reading this book, it's time for you to decide some things, too. First, you must decide whether you are willing to relinquish any biblically false beliefs you may have held prior to reading this book, such as the syncretism of evolutionary teaching with biblical teaching about the origin of life or the misapplication of predestination as God forcing us to be saved or lost against our will or the idea that once you are saved you can't abandon your faith as an apostate or anything else that may oppose what the Word of God actually says. Furthermore, you must decide whether you prefer the truth contained in God's Word, the Bible, or whether you prefer siding with your denominational teachings and guidelines, even though those teachings may contradict what the Bible says. In other words, are you more loyal to your denomination than you are to the Lord Jesus Christ and His Holy Word—the Bible? Finally, you must decide whether you want to help the Lord Jesus increase the citizenship of His Kingdom by sharing the Good News of the hope of His salvation with unbelieving members of your family and with everyone else you meet or simply keep bumbling along absorbed by self-interests until His eventual return, or until you die, whichever comes first.

Of course, by stating that last point I have just convicted my *own* conscience, since I'm not evangelizing as effectively as I should either! Nevertheless, I'm committing right now to begin sharing this Good News even more than I have since my own conversion. Time is most definitely running out, both for believers to labor in the field and for unbelievers to make up their minds as to whether they will accept this offer of salvation and begin living their lives for Christ. Since the future is so uncertain, this could very well be your last chance to make up your mind.

If you died before your next breath, where would *you* spend eternity? If you aren't certain beyond any doubt that you would spend it with Jesus Christ in His everlasting Kingdom of Love, Joy, and Peace, I plead with you to make your eternal destination sure right here and now. It's as simple as humbling yourself before God, admitting that you are a sinner in need of a Savior, and asking Jesus to apply His atoning blood to your soul for everlasting salvation. You might word your prayer something like this:

> **Dear Heavenly Father, I know I've sinned against You by violating Your commandments. Please forgive me! I turn away from my sins right now and accept Your Son Jesus Christ as my Lord and Savior. Please come into my heart by Your Holy Spirit this very moment, guide me into Your truth, and help me to live for You forevermore. Amen!**

My friend, if you just prayed that prayer with a humble and sincere heart, then Jesus Christ has just saved your soul and marked it for eternal salvation by giving you His Holy Spirit to be a guiding presence that lives within you. According to the Apostle Paul's writing in the Bible, the Holy Spirit is God's guarantee and seal upon the soul of every believer to prove that we belong to Him (2 Corinthians 1:21-22; 2 Corinthians 5:5; and Ephesians 1:11-14).

Now that you have made the decision to be a Christ follower, do not continue to practice the sins of your past (whatever they may be: lying, blaspheming, stealing, fornication, adultery, homosexuality, transgenderism, drunkenness, dabbling in spiritism, etc.). True repentance means you have forsaken your former lifestyle of sin once and forever. As Paul wrote to his young protégé, Timothy, "'Let everyone who names the name of Christ depart from iniquity'" (2 Timothy 2:19). While this does not mean we will never sin again, it *does* mean that we will live a godlier lifestyle than before we accepted Christ as our Lord and Savior. In fact, I like to say it this way: *before* we accepted Jesus, there was more sin than righteousness in our lives, but *after* we have accepted Jesus, there is more righteousness than sin in our lives. It's just that simple. I also like to say it this way: accepting Jesus as our Lord and Savior doesn't make us sinless, but it *does* make us sin *less*.

Next, find a local fellowship of other Christian believers who believe the Bible is the 100% inspired Word of God and get involved there with living the rest of your life on earth for God according to His Word, the Bible. It may prove challenging to find such a fellowship nowadays, but if you search diligently and ask for God's guidance, He will lead you to such a place. In fact, He might even call you to establish such a place yourself if one truly does not already exist near where you live. Be open to His leading and listen for His soft voice.

If you have come to accept and believe in Jesus Christ after reading this book, would you please share your decision with me in a note, whether by email or regular letter? It would give me such joy to know that I have played even a small part in leading you to the salvation of the LORD. My contact information is included at the end of this chapter.

Now, whether you were already a committed believer or have become one since reading this book, I pray God's richest blessings upon you in your future endeavors to serve Him faithfully. May He find us *all* faithful when He returns. ". . . Even so, come, Lord Jesus!" (Revelation 22:20).

Contact Information:

Rev. Michael L. White
P. O. Box 8277
Mobile, Alabama 36689-0277
MLWhite@parsonplace.com
https://books.parsonplace.com

ABOUT THE AUTHOR

Michael White has been preaching the Gospel of Jesus Christ since March 1978. He began his freelance writing career shortly after becoming a pastor in June 1984. You may learn more about him and his various ministries at parsonplace.com and his education and evangelism ministries at wellspringministries.org. You may also visit parsonplacepress.com/store for other titles he has published with his Christian publishing company, Parson Place Press.

Mike has been married to Ellen since 1981. They have two children, Amy and Josh, and three grandchildren, Makenzie, Connor, and Aiden.

Other Titles
from Parson Place Press
For more information, see www.parsonplacepress.com/store

Digital Evangelism (Second Edition)

by Michael L. White

ISBN 13: 978-0-9842163-2-1

Add digital evangelism to your repertoire of ministry skills

Seven Keys to Effective Prayer

by Michael L. White

ISBN 13: 978-0-9842163-8-3

Stop hindrances to your prayers now!

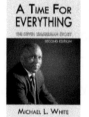

A Time For Everything (Second Edition)

by Michael White

ISBN 13: 978-0-9842163-6-9

Does God still work miracles today as He did in the Bible?

Lifelines

By Michael L. White

ISBN 13: 978-0-9888528-0-8

Inspiring poetry about God and His creation.

END NOTES

1 Merriam-Webster. *Righteous–Definition and More from the Free Merriam-Webster Dictionary.* https://www.merriam-webster.com/dictionary/righteous.

2 *Strong's Exhaustive Concordance.* Accessed within e-Sword version 13.0.0., 2021.

3 Merriam-Webster. *Generous–Definition and More from the Free Merriam-Webster Dictionary.* https://www.merriam-webster.com/dictionary/generous.

4 Robert Morris. *The End* Sermon Series. https://orders.theblessedlife.com/home.php?cat=9.

5 *Strong's Exhaustive Concordance.* Accessed within e-Sword version 13.0.0., 2021.

6 *Strong's Exhaustive Concordance.* Accessed within e-Sword version 13.0.0., 2021.

7 *Strong's Exhaustive Concordance,* G4690. Accessed within e-Sword version 13.0.0., 2021.

8 Online Latin Dictionary. https://www.online-latin-dictionary.com/english-latin-dictionary.php?parola=seed

9 Digital Hymnal. *Jesus Paid It All.* http://digitalhymnal.org/dhymn.cfm?hymnNumber=184

10 *Strong's Exhaustive Concordance.* Accessed within e-Sword version 13.0.0., 2021.

11 *Matthew Henry's Commentary on the Whole Bible,* by Matthew Henry. Published in 1708-1714. Accessed within e-Sword version 13.0.0., 2021.

12 *Fausset's Bible Dictionary,* by Andrew Robert Fausset. Published in 1888. Accessed within e-Sword version 13.0.0., 2021.

13 *Hitchcock's Bible Names* by Roswell D. Hitchcock. Published in 1874. Accessed within e-Sword version 13.0.0., 2021.

14 See notes and commentary in John Wesley's *Explanatory Notes on the Bible, The Companion Bible*, the *Ryrie Study Bible*, and the *Schofield Bible*. Accessed within e-Sword version 13.0.0., 2021.

15 William Shakespeare. "Romeo and Juliet." In *The Complete Works of William Shakespeare*, by William George Clark, & William Aldis Wright, 720. London: Parragon Publishing, 2000.

16 *Preface* of the *Holy Bible, New King James Version*, vi. Nashville: Thomas Nelson Publishers, 1982.

17 *Smith's Bible Dictionary* by William Smith. Accessed within e-Sword version 13.0.0., 2021.

18 *Strong's Exhaustive Concordance.* Accessed within e-Sword version 13.0.0., 2021.

19 *International Standard Bible Encyclopedia.* Accessed within e-Sword version 13.0.0., 2021.

20 This is the 1769 King James Version of the Holy Bible (also known as the Authorized Version) with the words of Jesus Christ in red. Includes Strong's numbers for looking up the original Hebrew or Greek word in a lexicon. Derivative Work, Copyright © 2002-2019 by Rick Meyers. All rights reserved.

21 *Strong's Exhaustive Concordance*. Accessed within e-Sword version 13.0.0., 2021.

22 *Strong's Exhaustive Concordance*. Accessed within e-Sword version 13.0.0., 2021.

23 Perry Stone. *The Noah Code*, DVD. Cleveland, TN: Voice of Evangelism, 2013. Start at the 4:57 mark.

24 Paul Taylor. *The Six Days of Genesis*, 135. Green Forest, AR: Master Books, 2007.

25 Calculated by searching on the word "salvation" in the KJV+, noting the total number of occurrences, and then searching on the term "H3444" from *Strong's Exhaustive Concordance* and noting the total number of occurrences. Accessed within e-Sword version 13.0.0, 2021.

26 W. E. Vine, Merrill F. Unger, and William White, Jr. *Vine's Complete Expository Dictionary of Old and New Testament Words*. Accessed within e-Sword version 13.0.0., 2021.

27 *Strong's Exhaustive Concordance*. Accessed within e-Sword version 13.0.0., 2021.

28 *Strong's Exhaustive Concordance*. Accessed within e-Sword version 13.0.0., 2021.

29 *Strong's Exhaustive Concordance*. Accessed within e-Sword version 13.0.0., 2021.

30 Here I have used the following English translations of the Bible which I have installed in e-Sword 13.0.0: *The American*

Standard Version; the 1965 *Bible in Basic English*; the *Bishops Bible* (which actually predates the 1611 King James Version); the *Contemporary English Version*; the *Complete Jewish Bible*; the *English Standard Version*; the *Geneva Bible* (which also predates the 1611 King James Version); the *Good News Bible* (also called the *Good News Translation* or *Today's English Version*); the *Holman Christian Standard Bible*; the 1769 *King James Version*; the *Literal Translation of the Holy Bible*; the *Modern King James Version*; the *New American Standard Bible*; the *New King James Version*; and the 1898 publication of *Young's Literal Translation*.

31 *Strong's Exhaustive Concordance*. Accessed within e-Sword version 13.0.0., 2021.

32 Merriam-Webster. *Fate–Definition and More from the Free Merriam-Webster Dictionary*. https://www.merriam-webster.com/dictionary/fate.

33 Ask.com. *How Many Verses Are There in the Bible?* http://www.ask.com/question/how-many-verses-are-there-in-the-bible.

34 Merriam-Webster. *Blasphemy–Definition and More from the Free Merriam-Webster Dictionary*. https://www.merriam-webster.com/dictionary/blasphemy.

35 Merriam-Webster. *Unpardonable–Defintion and More from the Free Merriam-Webster Dictionary*. https://www.merriam-webster.com/dictionary/unpardonable.

36 Merriam-Webster. *Pardonable–Definition and More from the Free Merriam-Webster Dictionary*. https://www.merriam-webster.com/dictionary/pardonable.

37 *Strong's Exhaustive Concordance*. Accessed within e-Sword version 13.0.0., 2021.

38 *Strong's Exhaustive Concordance.* Accessed within e-Sword version 13.0.0., 2021.

39 *Thayer's Greek Definitions,* originally published in 1886 & 1889. Accessed within e-Sword version 13.0.0, 2021.

40 Merriam-Webster. *Apostasy—Definition and More from the Free Merriam-Webster Dictionary.* https://www.merriam-webster.com/dictionary/apostasy.

41 *Thayer's Greek Definitions,* originally published in 1886 & 1889. Accessed within e-Sword version 13.0.0., 2021.

42 Go to https://www.e-sword.net/ to download this software for free. However, you will need to download additional resources, such as commentaries, Bible dictionaries, etc., after completing the initial installation of the e-Sword software. These are available for both free and paid, depending on your choices, but you are not required to purchase anything. You may also find download links for both Apple and Android handheld devices, but each of these costs a small fee, which is well worth the expense for all that is included. There are also a variety of products available for purchase for integration into the e-Sword software, which may be ordered for immediate download from the site, eStudySource, found at https://www.estudysource.com/

43 *Strong's Exhaustive Concordance.* Accessed within e-Sword version 13.0.0., 2021.

44 Merriam-Webster. *Abundant—Definition and More from the Free Merriam-Webster Dictionary.* https://www.merriam-webster.com/dictionary/abundant.

45 *Amazing Grace.* The final verse of this hymn (which is quoted in this reference) is attributed to an anonymous author, rather than the composer, John Newton. Complete lyrics to this hymn may be found in any hymnal or on various Websites, including Hymnal.net at: https://www.hymnal.net/en/hymn/h/313

[46] *Strong's Exhaustive Concordance.* Accessed within e-Sword version 13.0.0., 2021.

[47] W. E. Vine, Merrill F. Unger, and William White, Jr. *Vine's Complete Expository Dictionary of Old and New Testament Words.* e-Sword version 13.0.0., 2021.

[48] *Strong's Exhaustive Concordance.* Accessed within e-Sword version 13.0.0., 2021.

[49] *Thayer's Greek Definitions.* Accessed within e-Sword version 13.0.0., 2021.

[50] In a sermon delivered on Christmas morning, 2013, Pope Francis issued a grave misinterpretation and misapplication of the Scriptures regarding the blood of Jesus Christ and His Plan of Redemption for human souls. Whereas the blood of Jesus did indeed pay for the sins of *all* humanity (per John 3:16-18 and Hebrews 9:11-15 & 10:10), it does not save *any* human soul until that soul believes (i.e., trusts) in Him for this salvation (John 3:18; 8:24; & 14:6). While one Roman Catholic Website attempted to draw a distinction between redemption and salvation and make Pope Francis say something more in line with Roman Catholic doctrine (which he didn't actually say), we should let his words speak for themselves. Following are just a few URLs for you to use in further reading on this incident, including a response from an atheist at the Richard Dawkins Foundation:

- http://www.catholicvote.org/what-pope-francis-really-said-about-atheists/
- http://www.catholic.org/hf/faith/story.php?id= 51077
- http://www.christiancentury.org/article/2013-12/pope-francis-script-christmas-nod-atheists-part-pattern
- http://www.richarddawkins.net/news_articles/2013/10/7/that-s-an-atheist-thing-to-do-pope-francis.

Milton Keynes UK
Ingram Content Group UK Ltd.
UKHW020925220424
441551UK00017B/1293